GRAPHIC MODERN HISTORY: WORLD WAR I

LAWRENCE OF ARABIA AND THE MIDDLE EAST AND AFRICA

By Gary Jeffrey & Illustrated by Nick Spender

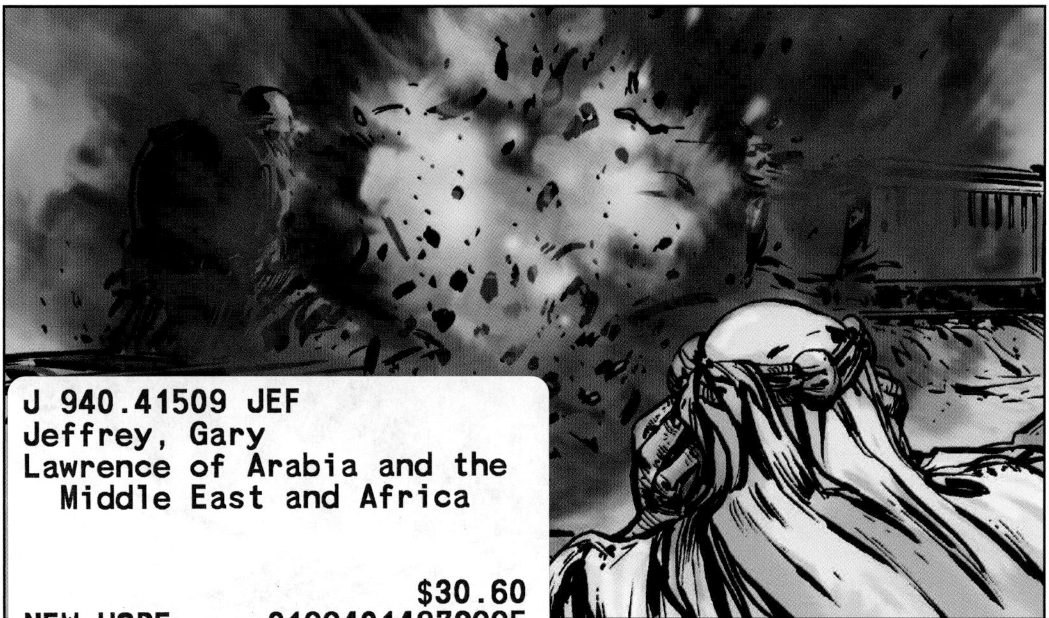

Crabtree Publishing Company
www.crabtreebooks.com

Crabtree Publishing Company

www.crabtreebooks.com

Created and produced by:
David West Children's Books

Project development, design, and concept:
David West Children's Books

Author and designer: Gary Jeffrey

Illustrator: Nick Spender

Editor: Lynn Peppas

Proofreader: Kelly McNiven

Project coordinator: Kathy Middleton

Print and production coordinator:
Katherine Berti

Prepress technician: Katherine Berti

Photographs: p7t, m, Bundesarchiv

Library and Archives Canada Cataloguing in Publication

Jeffrey, Gary
    Lawrence of Arabia and the Middle East and Africa /
Gary Jeffrey; illustrated by Nick Spender.

(Graphic modern history : World War I)
Includes index.
Issued also in electronic formats.
ISBN 978-0-7787-0912-1 (bound).
--ISBN 978-0-7787-0918-3 (pbk.)

        1. Lawrence, T. E. (Thomas Edward), 1888-1935--Juvenile
literature. 2. Lawrence, T. E. (Thomas Edward), 1888-1935--
Comic books, strips, etc. 3. World War, 1914-1918--Campaigns-
-Arab countries--Juvenile literature. 4. World War, 1914-1918--
Campaigns--Arab countries--Comic books, strips, etc. 5.
Graphic novels. I. Spender, Nik II. Title. III. Series: Jeffrey,
Gary. Graphic modern history. World War I.

D568.4.J35 2013   j940.4'156   C2013-901420-9

Library of Congress Cataloging-in-Publication Data

Jeffrey, Gary.
  Lawrence of Arabia and the Middle East and Africa / Gary
Jeffrey & illustrated by Nick Spender.
        pages cm. -- (Graphic modern history: World War I)
  Includes index.
  ISBN 978-0-7787-0912-1 (reinforced library binding)
-- ISBN 978-0-7787-0918-3 (pbk.) -- ISBN 978-1-4271-9255-4
(electronic pdf) -- ISBN 978-1-4271-9179-3 (electronic html)
  1. Lawrence, T. E. (Thomas Edward), 1888-1935--Comic books,
strips, etc. 2. Lawrence, T. E. (Thomas Edward), 1888-1935--
Juvenile literature. 3. World War, 1914-1918--Campaigns--
Middle East--Comic books, strips, etc. 4. World War, 1914-1918--
Campaigns--Middle East--Juvenile literature. 5. Soldiers--Great
Britain--Biography--Comic books, strips, etc. 6. Soldiers--Great
Britain--Biography--Juvenile literature. 7. Graphic novels. I.
Spender, Nik, illustrator. II. Title.

  D568.4.L45J44 2013
  940.4'15092--dc23

                                              2013007630

Crabtree Publishing Company

www.crabtreebooks.com   1-800-387-7650

Printed in the U.S.A./042013/SX20130306

Published in Canada
Crabtree Publishing
616 Welland Ave.
St. Catharines, Ontario
L2M 5V6

Published in the United States
Crabtree Publishing
PMB 59051
350 Fifth Avenue, 59th Floor
New York, New York 10118

Published in the United Kingdom
Crabtree Publishing
Maritime House
Basin Road North, Hove
BN41 1WR

Published in Australia
Crabtree Publishing
3 Charles Street
Coburg North
VIC 3058

CONTENTS

CLASH OF EMPIRES

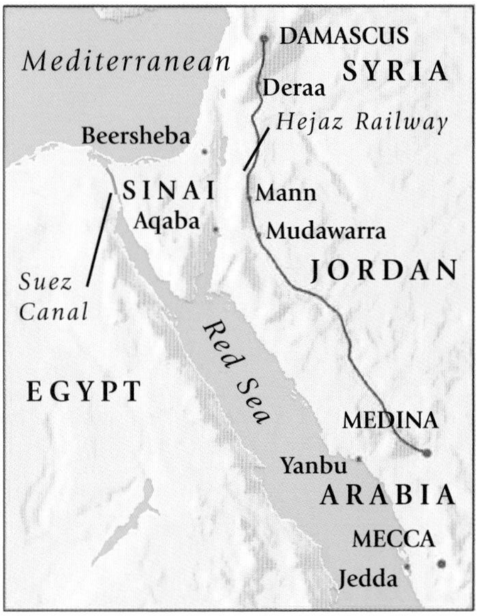
DAMASCUS
Mediterranean
SYRIA
Deraa
Hejaz Railway
Beersheba
SINAI
Mann
Aqaba
Mudawarra
JORDAN
Suez Canal
Red Sea
EGYPT
MEDINA
Yanbu
ARABIA
MECCA
Jedda

The Turkish Ottoman Empire had ruled over Palestine and Arabia for nearly 500 years. When the Ottomans entered the war on the side of the Central Powers, the British Empire had to open a front to protect the vital waterway of the Suez Canal.

The 700-mile (1,126 km) Hejaz Railway joined Ottoman Syria with Ottoman Jordan and ran into Arabia.

Battle for the Canal

The Turks decided to attack the Suez Canal from the east, across the Sinai Desert. Capturing the canal would cut Britain's direct route to her colonies and perhaps encourage the Egyptian Arabs to revolt against the British.

After a ten-day trek Turkish men from two divisions boarded inflatable boats on the eastern bank of the canal. British machine gun fire destroyed them. Those who got across were taken prisoner. The attack was aborted. The canal was safe for now.

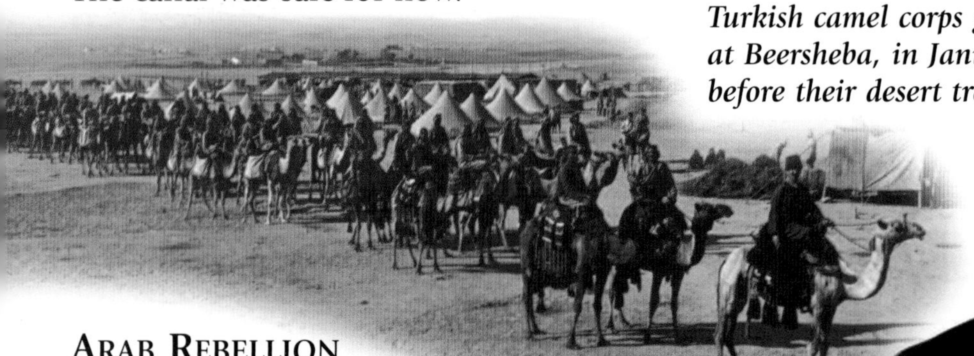

Turkish camel corps gathered at Beersheba, in January 1915, before their desert trek.

Arab Rebellion

The Young Turks, who had come to power in 1908, were set on "turkifying" the Middle East. When Arab nationalists were executed in 1915, Sherif Hussein of Mecca began a rebellion, capturing Mecca, Yanbu, and Jedda.

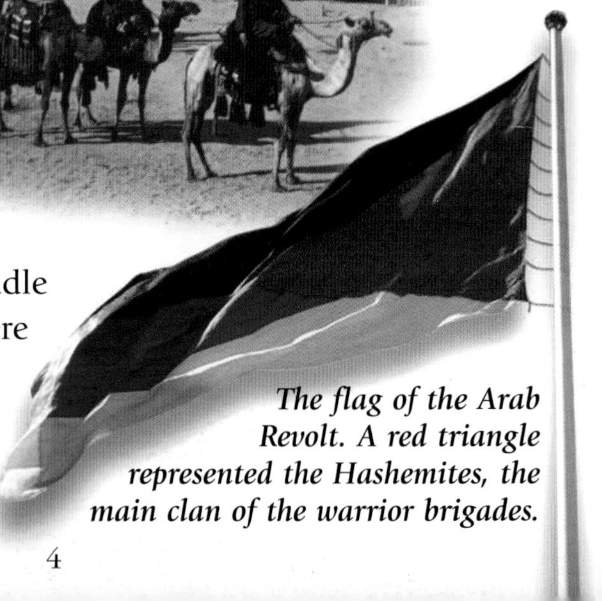

The flag of the Arab Revolt. A red triangle represented the Hashemites, the main clan of the warrior brigades.

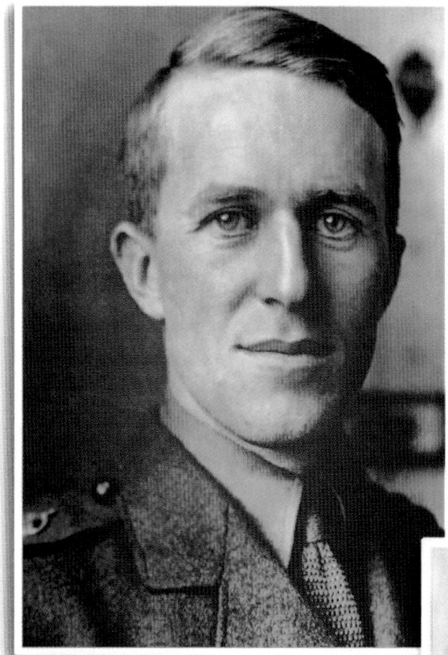

Fixers

When the Arab rebellion began, in June 1916, British advisers were sent to offer help and guidance. A staff officer from Military Intelligence in Cairo, Captain T. E. Lawrence, knew the campaign area well and spoke fluent Arabic. Having an affinity with the Arabs, Lawrence had to pick one of Sherif Hussein's sons to lead an aggressive campaign against the Turks. Emir (prince) Abdulla was thought by Lawrence to be "too clever," however his brother, Emir Feisal, "had the necessary fire."

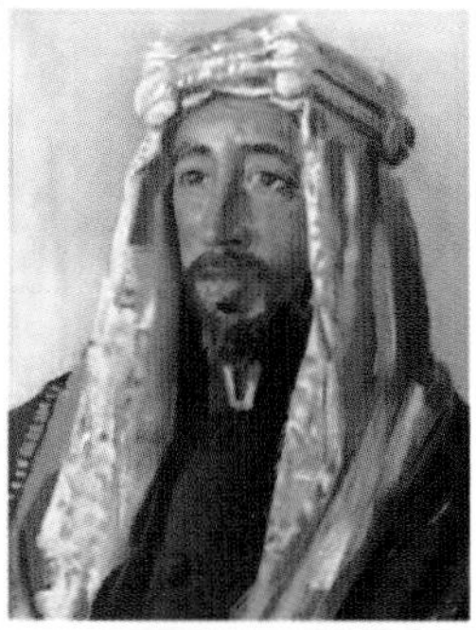

Lawrence (above) decided to supply Emir Feisal (right) and his Northern Arab Army with the bulk of British aid.

First Actions

Most of Feisal's 6,000 Arab troops were nomads, called Bedouin. The strong Turkish garrison, or military post, at Medina had been unsuccessfully attacked twice, and with deadly losses. The Turks came out to pursue the Arabs and retake Yanbu. Fierce fire from British warships in the Red Sea defeated them. Lawrence was then ordered to begin attacks on the Hejaz Railway.

In Africa, by 1916, nearly all the recently established German colonies had been overrun by superior Allied forces, but not East Africa.

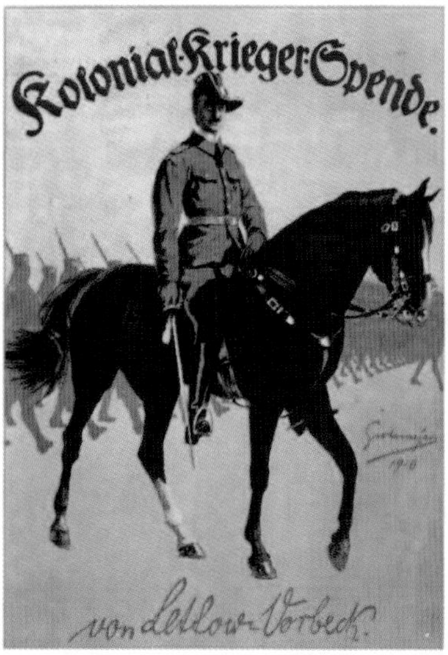
Kolonial-Krieger-Spende.
von Lettow-Vorbeck

In German East Africa Colonel Lettow-Vorbeck resisted a British invasion by taking his army to the hills.

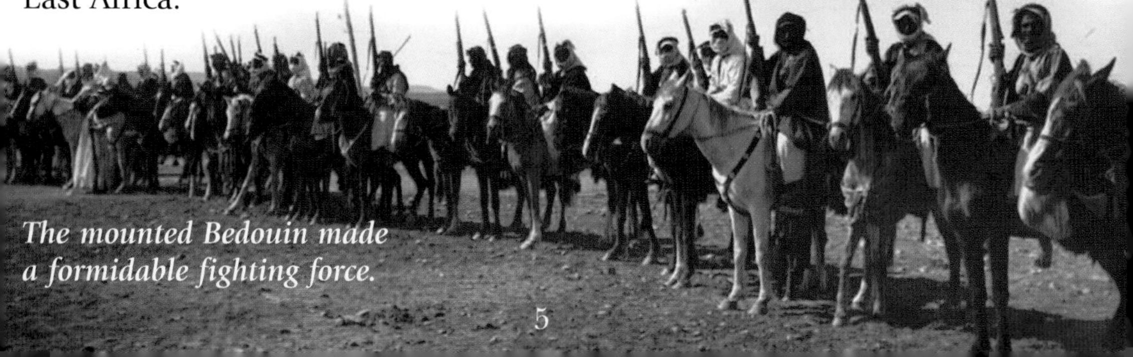

The mounted Bedouin made a formidable fighting force.

DESERT RAIDERS

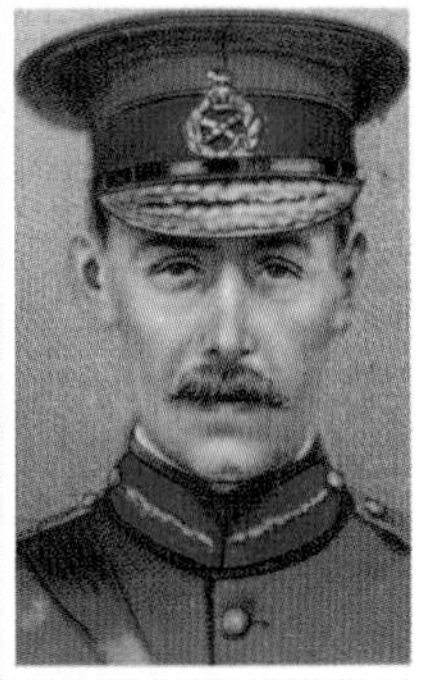

General Sir A. Murray

By January 1917, the Allied Egyptian Expeditionary Force (EEF) had crossed the desert to capture Rafa, in Sinai. The Suez Canal was now safe. The key city of Gaza in Palestine was less than one day's march away. General Archibald Murray made plans to attack it.

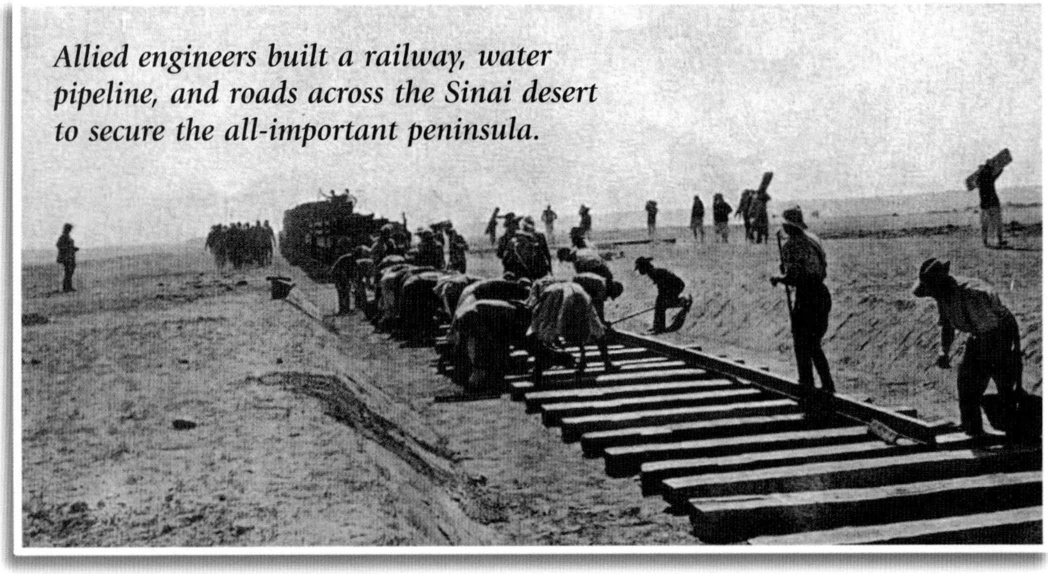

Allied engineers built a railway, water pipeline, and roads across the Sinai desert to secure the all-important peninsula.

THE TAKING OF AQABA

Lawrence and his Arabs spent the spring of 1917 blowing up parts of the Hejaz Railway. Feisal was considering an all-out attack on Medina, but Lawrence convinced him that threatening the railway would use up more Turkish troops, and for little risk.

Lawrence had another target in mind—the small port of Aqaba on the Red Sea. He felt that taking Aqaba would increase awareness of the Arab cause in the war.

After trekking through the Nefud desert Lawrence, Auda, and their small band staged a surprise charge against the Turkish strong point. In a staggering victory, over 600 Turks were killed or captured. Only two Arabs were lost.

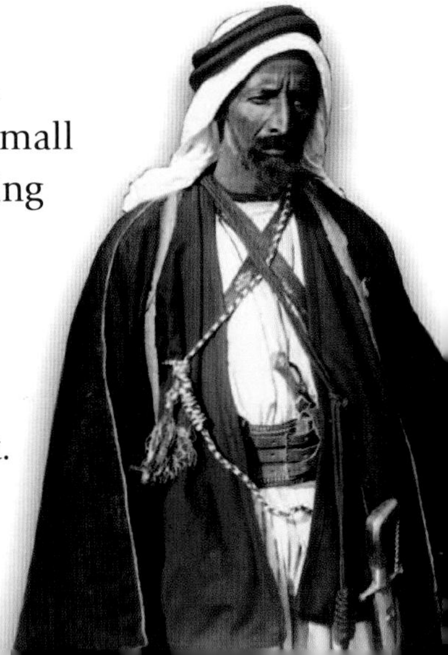

To take Aqaba, Lawrence secured the help of Auda ibu Tayi, a legendary fighter and leader of the Howeitat tribe.

War of the Askaris

In East Africa Lettow-Vorbeck was operating in what is now modern day Tanzania. He had 1,800 Germans, plus 12,000 Askaris, but was vastly outnumbered in any battles. Lettow-Vorbeck hoped his hit-and-run guerilla tactics would divert Allied troops from the Western Front. He was very successful at first, which frustrated the Allies.

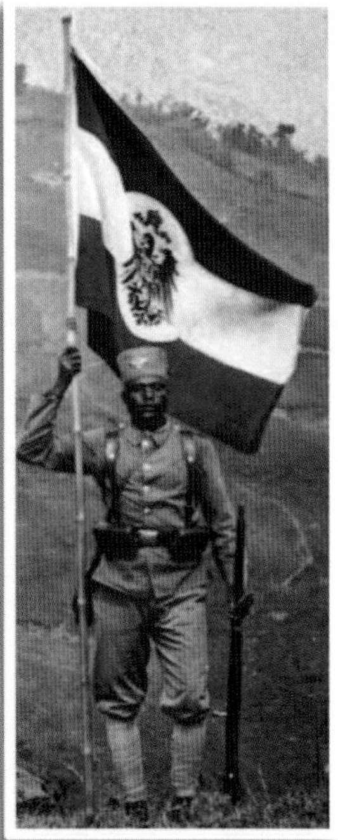

An Askari was a locally-recruited soldier, here a German African.

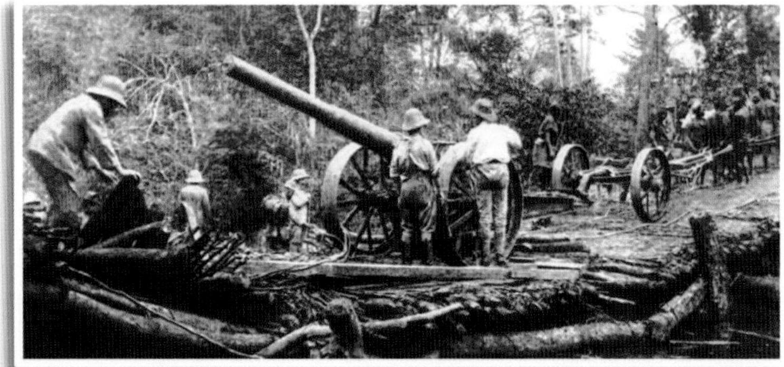

German "schutztruppe," or colonial soldiers, move guns in the jungles of East Africa.

The Battles for Gaza

The first attack on Gaza was on March 26, 1917. Infantry, supported by Australian and New Zealand (ANZAC) horsemen, succeeded in forcing back the Turkish line. A mix-up overnight saw the Allied troops withdraw. A second attempt in April broke up against much-strengthened Turkish defenses.

"Jerusalem by Christmas"

Murray was replaced by General Allenby, who reorganized the EEF and carefully prepared for another assault. His plan was to take Beersheba first, by secretly moving 40,000 infantry and ANZAC cavalry across harsh terrain.

General Edmund Allenby

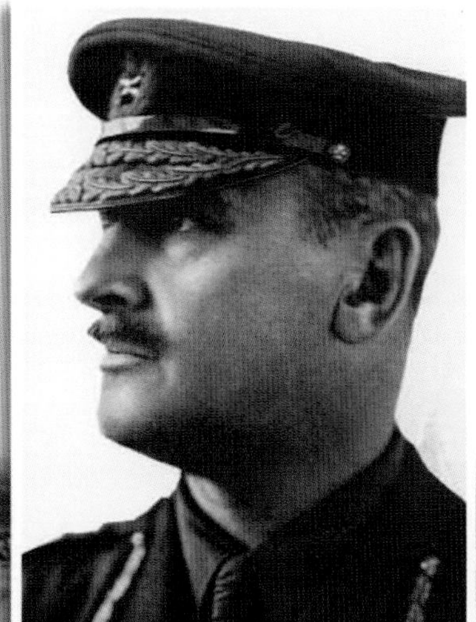

Turkish gunners defend the Gaza line.

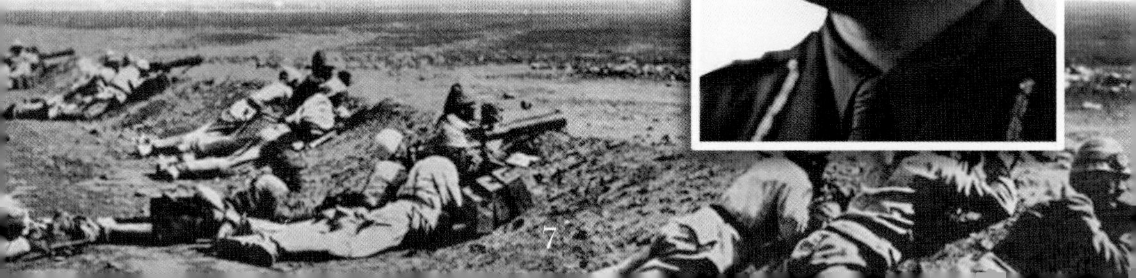

AN ATTACK ON THE HEJAZ RAILWAY

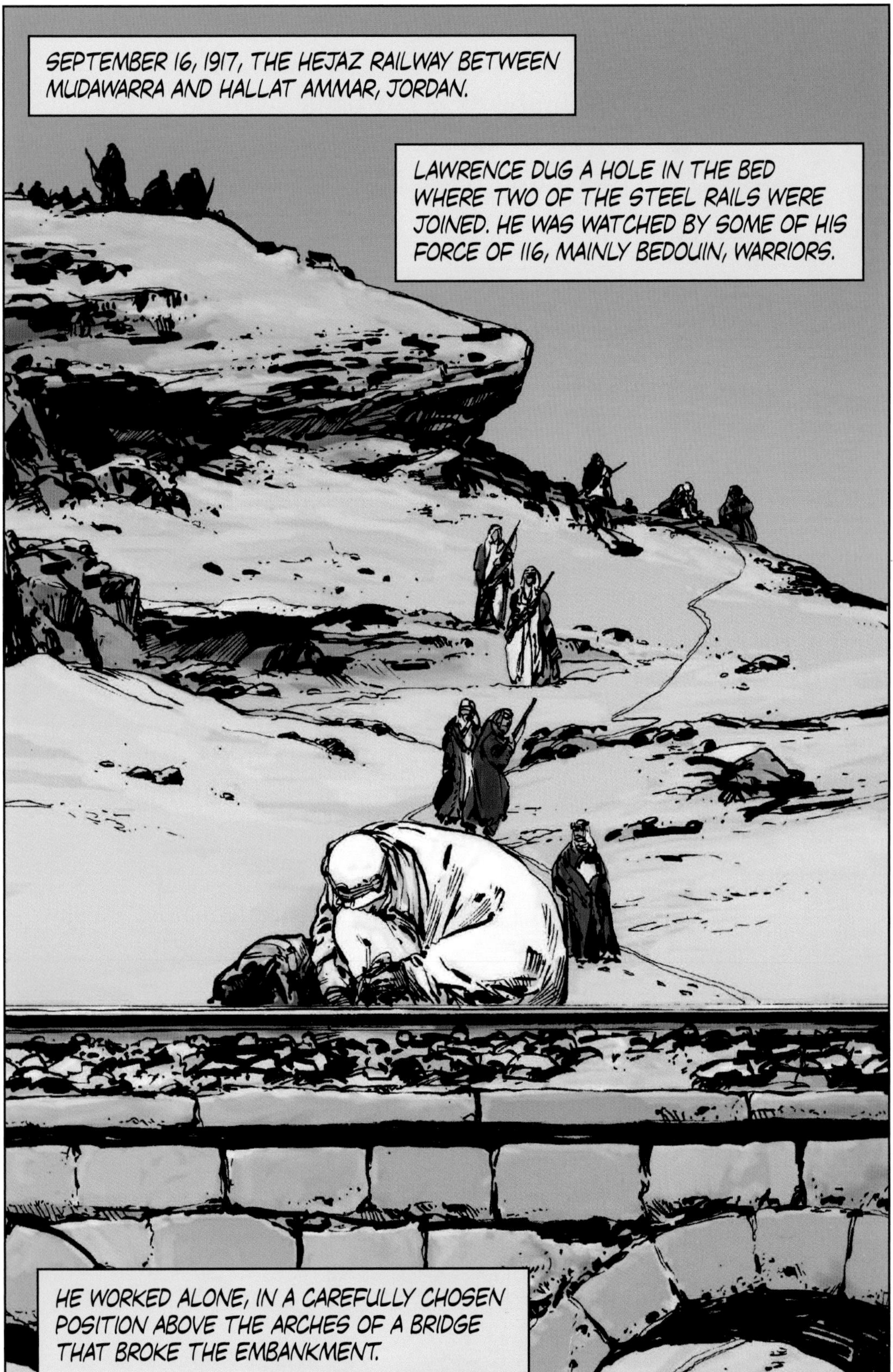
SEPTEMBER 16, 1917, THE HEJAZ RAILWAY BETWEEN MUDAWARRA AND HALLAT AMMAR, JORDAN.
LAWRENCE DUG A HOLE IN THE BED WHERE TWO OF THE STEEL RAILS WERE JOINED. HE WAS WATCHED BY SOME OF HIS FORCE OF 116, MAINLY BEDOUIN, WARRIORS.
HE WORKED ALONE, IN A CAREFULLY CHOSEN POSITION ABOVE THE ARCHES OF A BRIDGE THAT BROKE THE EMBANKMENT.

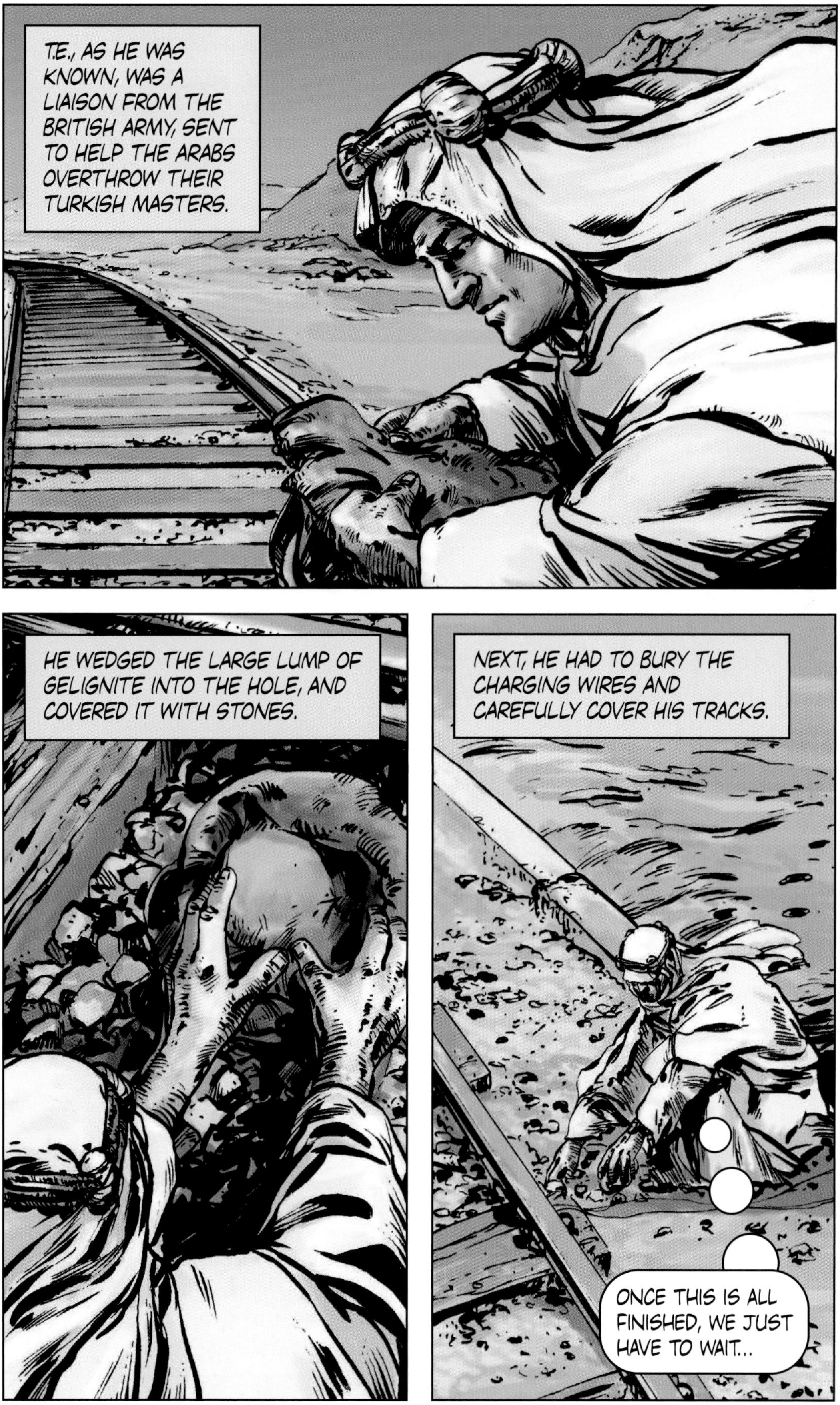
T.E., AS HE WAS KNOWN, WAS A LIAISON FROM THE BRITISH ARMY, SENT TO HELP THE ARABS OVERTHROW THEIR TURKISH MASTERS.
HE WEDGED THE LARGE LUMP OF GELIGNITE INTO THE HOLE, AND COVERED IT WITH STONES.
NEXT, HE HAD TO BURY THE CHARGING WIRES AND CAREFULLY COVER HIS TRACKS.
ONCE THIS IS ALL FINISHED, WE JUST HAVE TO WAIT...

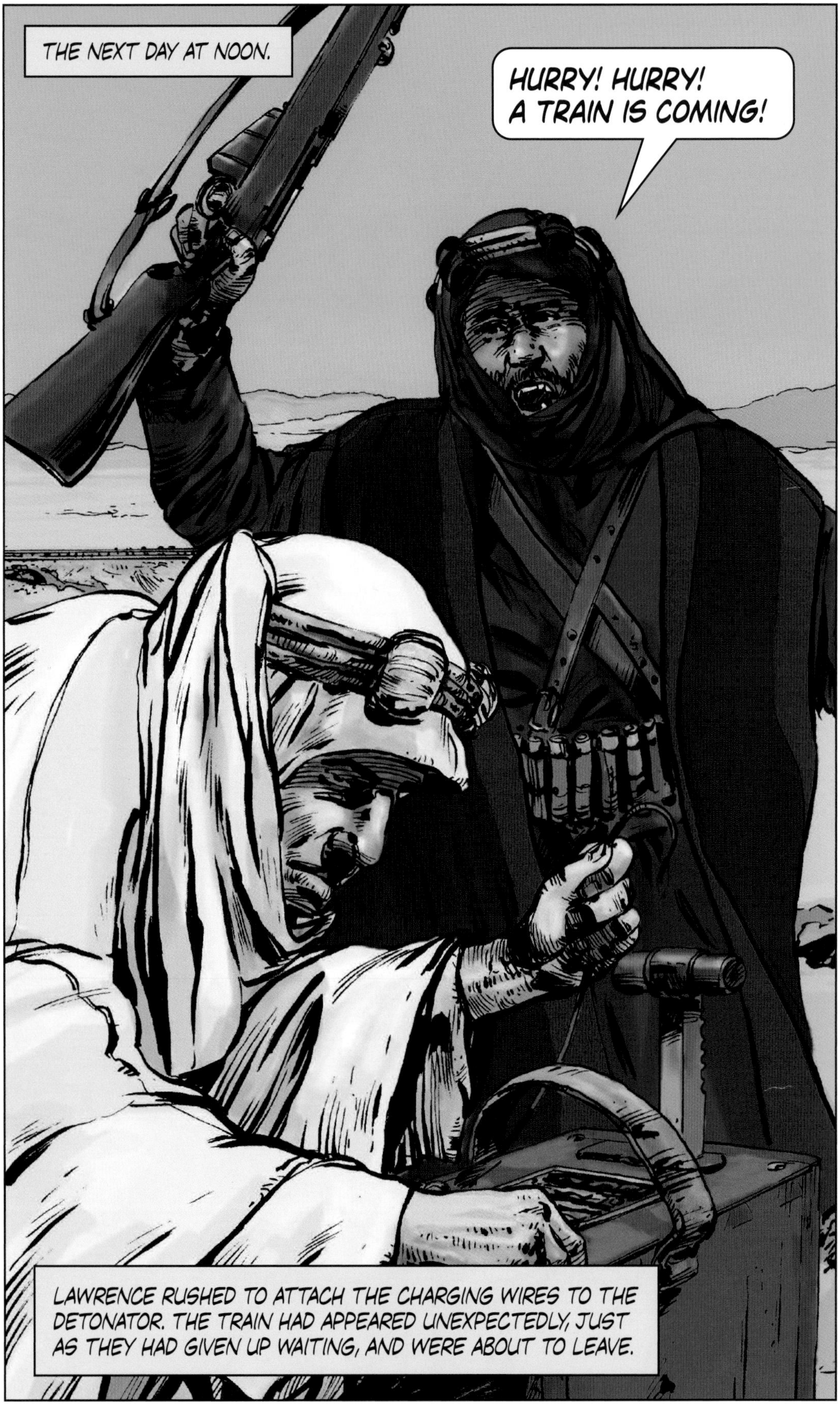
THE NEXT DAY AT NOON.
HURRY! HURRY! A TRAIN IS COMING!
LAWRENCE RUSHED TO ATTACH THE CHARGING WIRES TO THE DETONATOR. THE TRAIN HAD APPEARED UNEXPECTEDLY, JUST AS THEY HAD GIVEN UP WAITING, AND WERE ABOUT TO LEAVE.

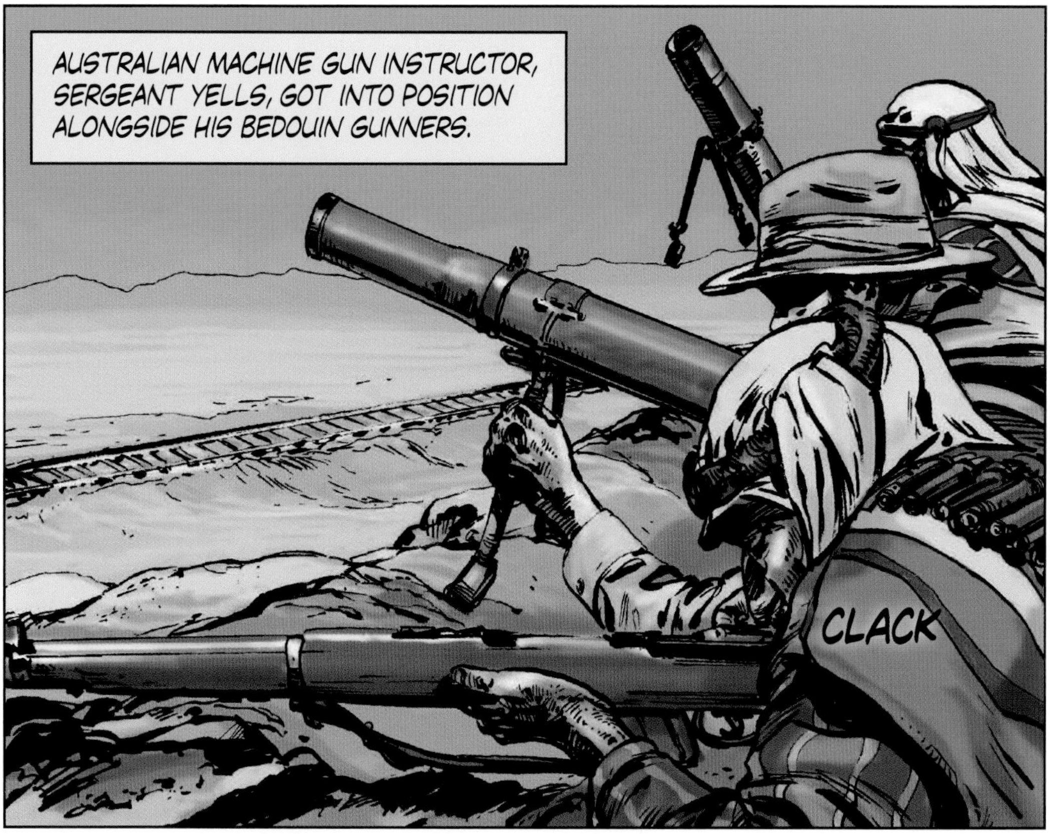
AUSTRALIAN MACHINE GUN INSTRUCTOR, SERGEANT YELLS, GOT INTO POSITION ALONGSIDE HIS BEDOUIN GUNNERS.
CLACK

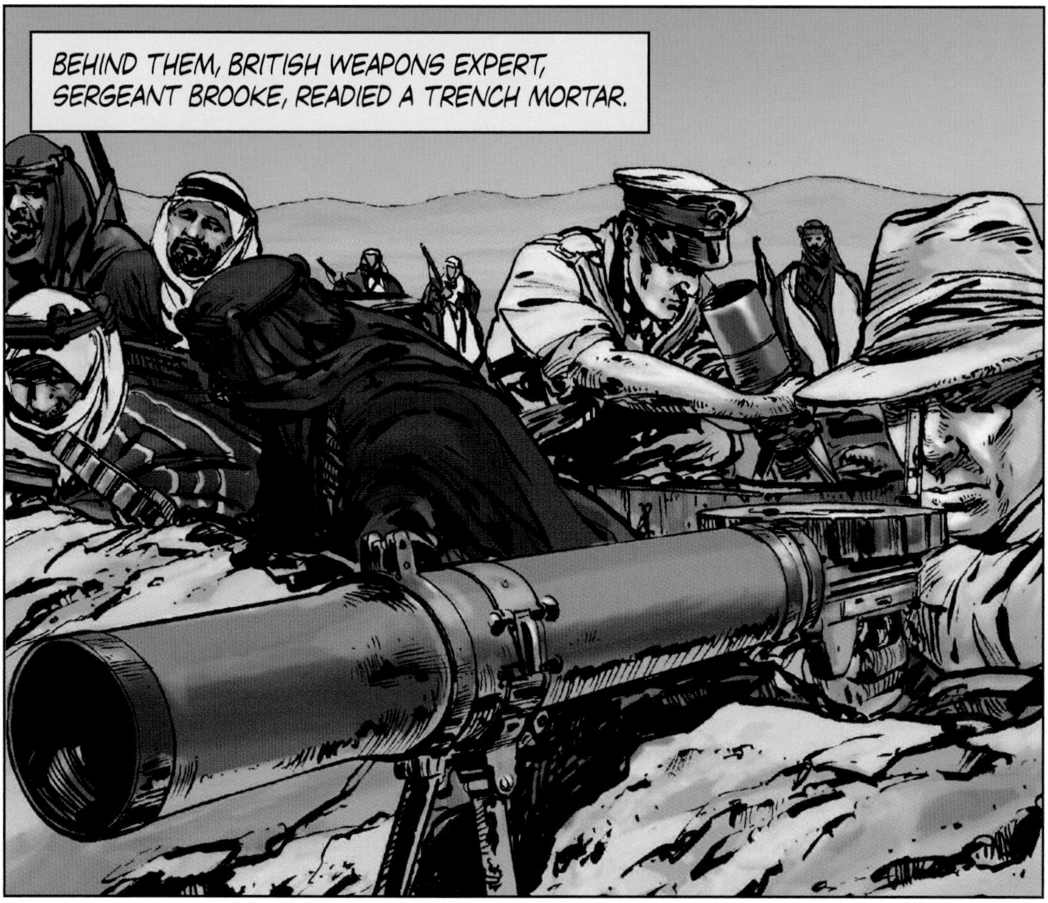
BEHIND THEM, BRITISH WEAPONS EXPERT, SERGEANT BROOKE, READIED A TRENCH MORTAR.

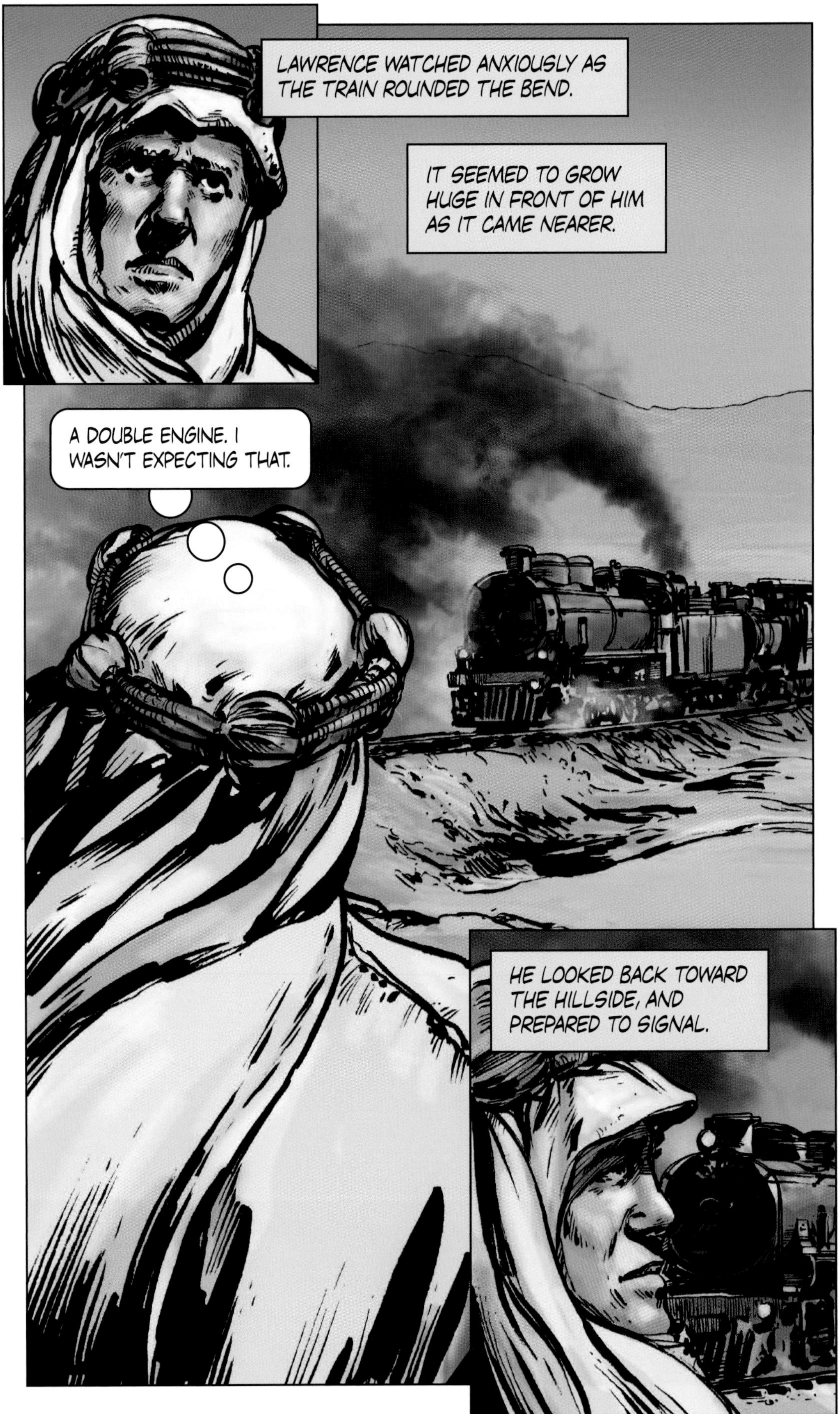
LAWRENCE WATCHED ANXIOUSLY AS THE TRAIN ROUNDED THE BEND.
IT SEEMED TO GROW HUGE IN FRONT OF HIM AS IT CAME NEARER.
A DOUBLE ENGINE. I WASN'T EXPECTING THAT.
HE LOOKED BACK TOWARD THE HILLSIDE, AND PREPARED TO SIGNAL.

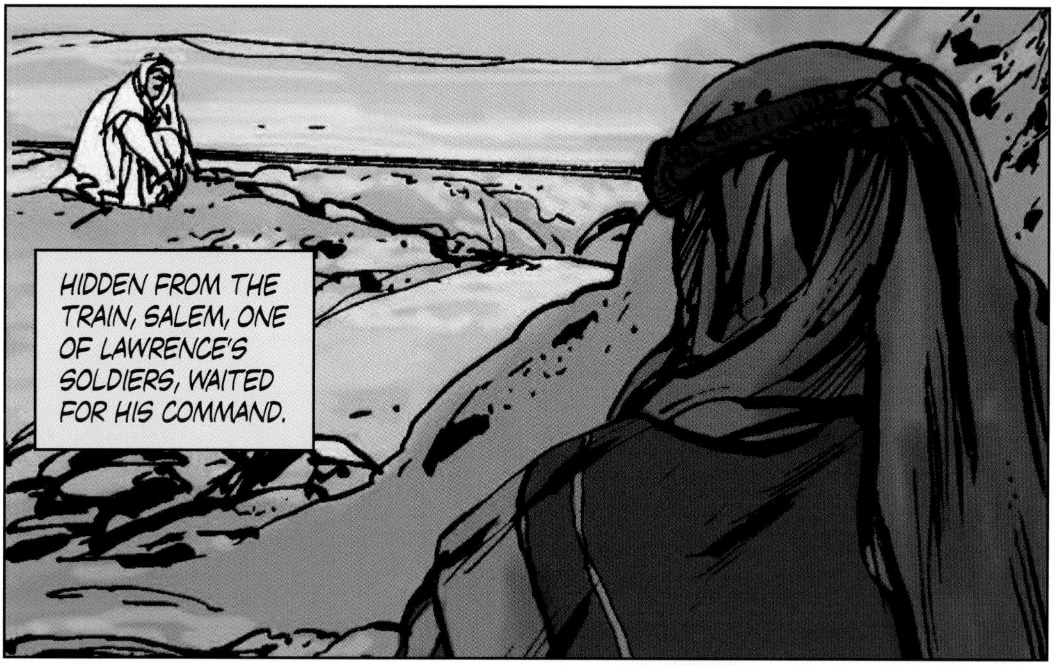
HIDDEN FROM THE TRAIN, SALEM, ONE OF LAWRENCE'S SOLDIERS, WAITED FOR HIS COMMAND.

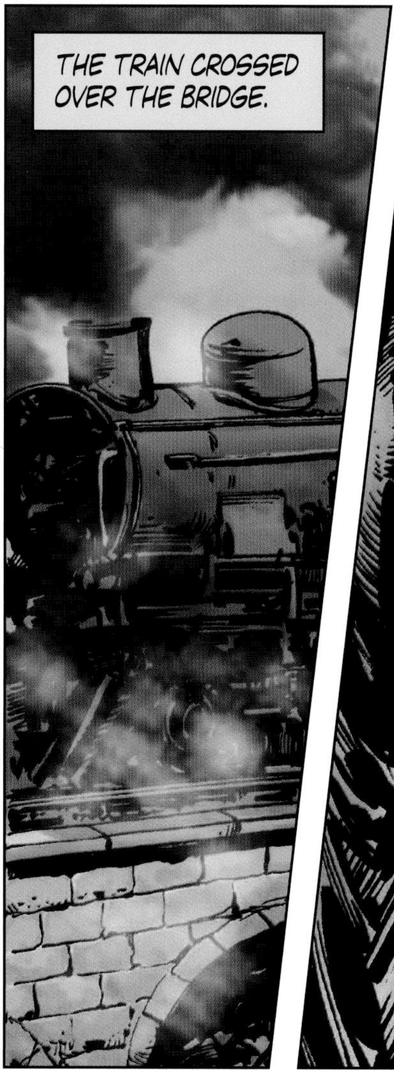
THE TRAIN CROSSED OVER THE BRIDGE.

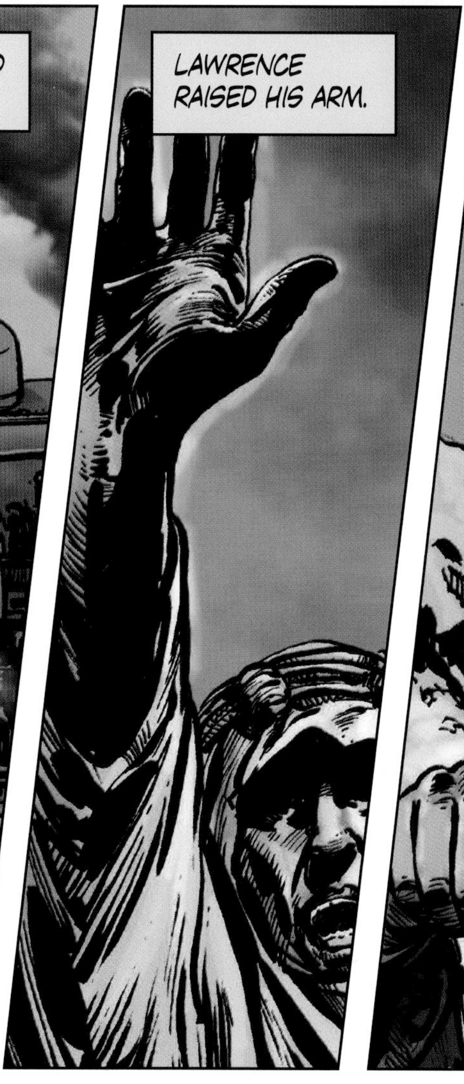
LAWRENCE RAISED HIS ARM.

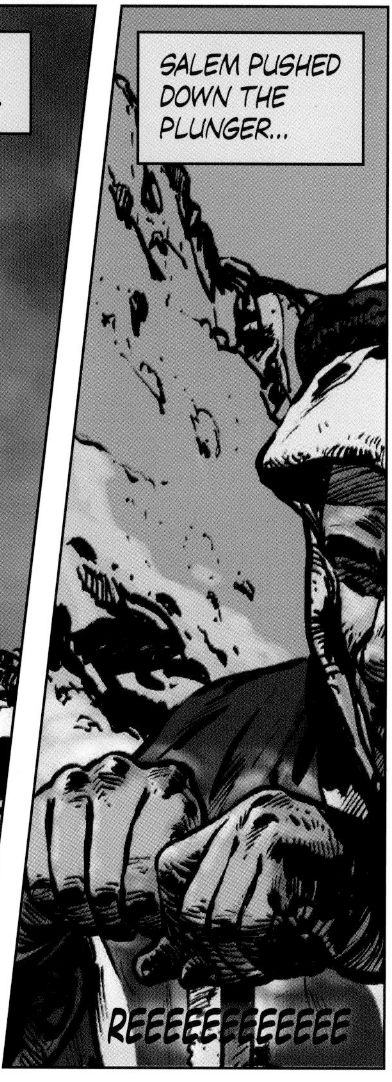
SALEM PUSHED DOWN THE PLUNGER...
REEEEEEEEEEEE

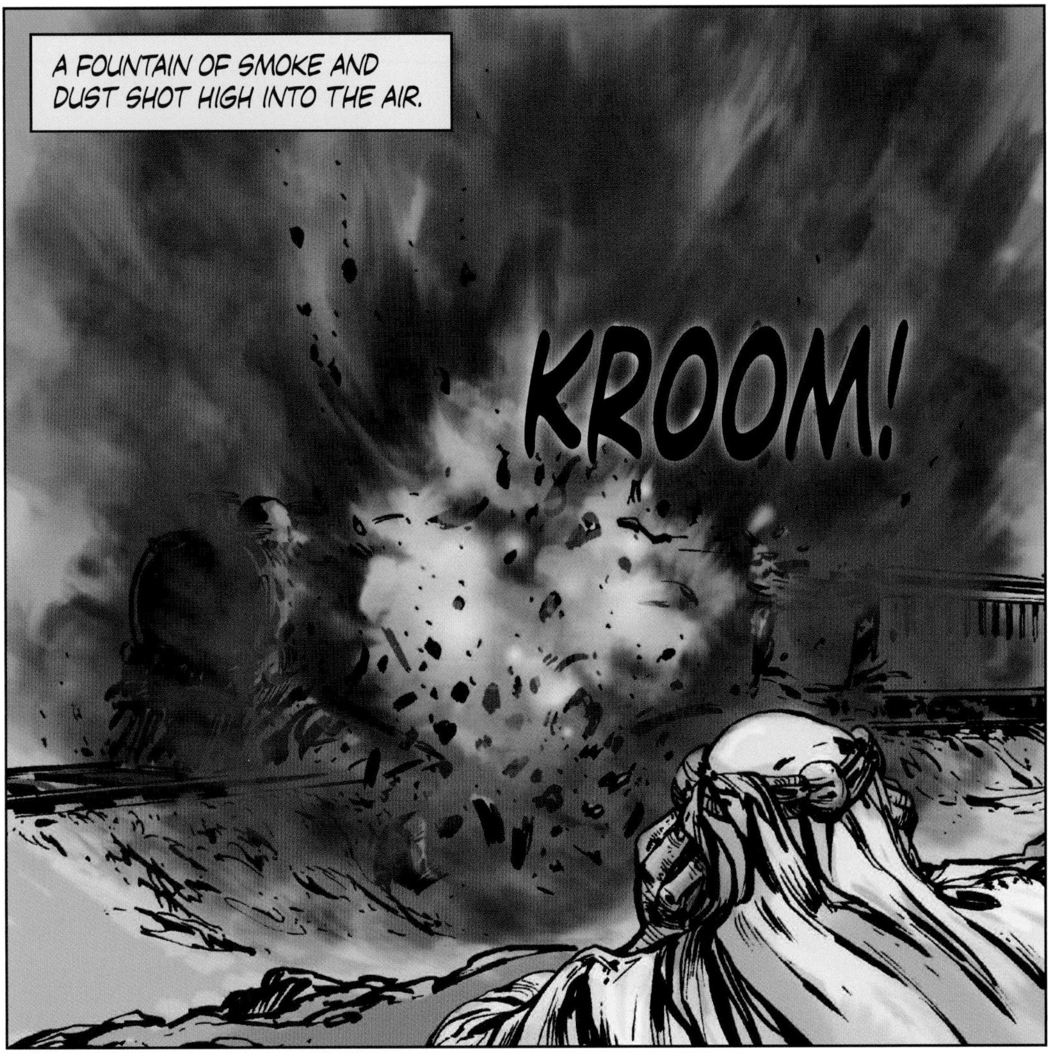
A FOUNTAIN OF SMOKE AND DUST SHOT HIGH INTO THE AIR.
KROOM!

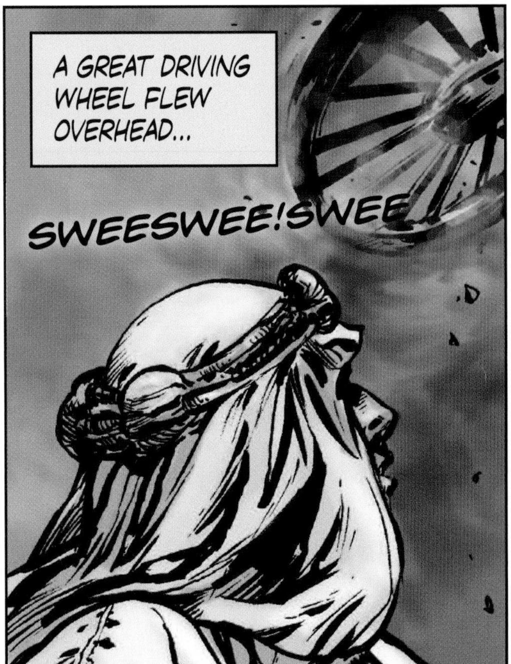
A GREAT DRIVING WHEEL FLEW OVERHEAD...
SWEESWEE!SWEE

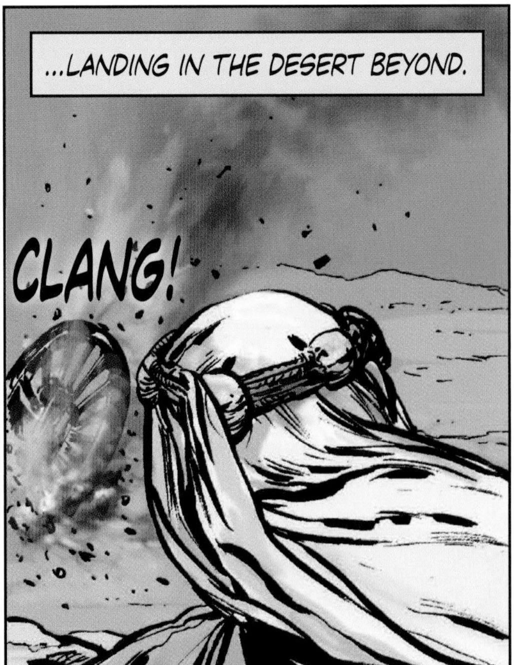
...LANDING IN THE DESERT BEYOND.
CLANG!

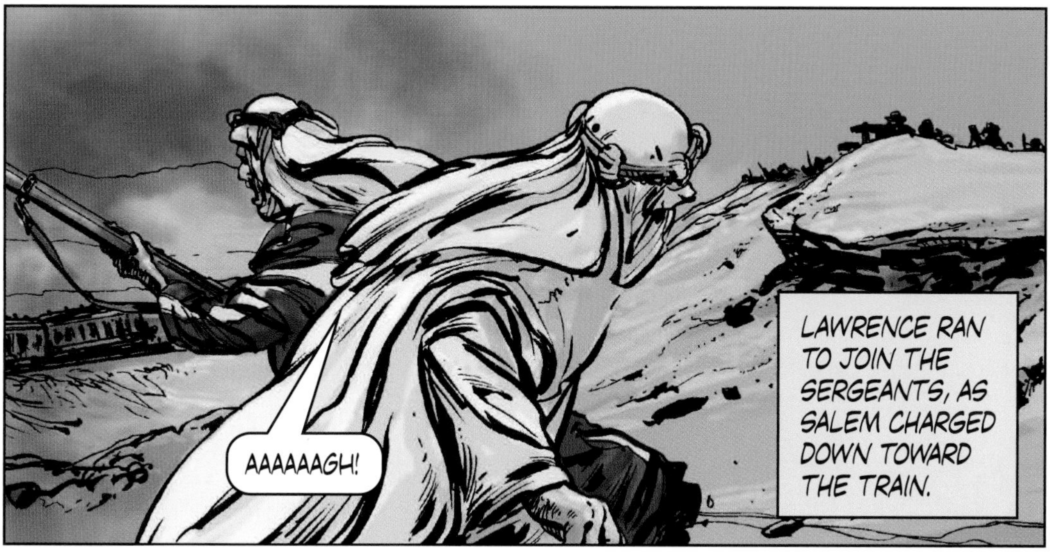
AAAAAAGH!
LAWRENCE RAN TO JOIN THE SERGEANTS, AS SALEM CHARGED DOWN TOWARD THE TRAIN.

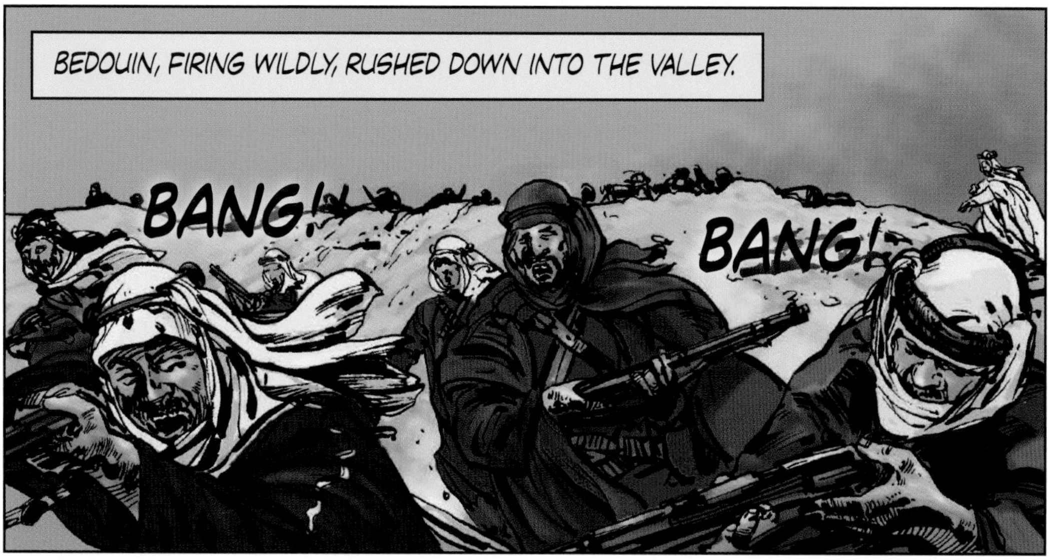
BEDOUIN, FIRING WILDLY, RUSHED DOWN INTO THE VALLEY.
BANG!
BANG!

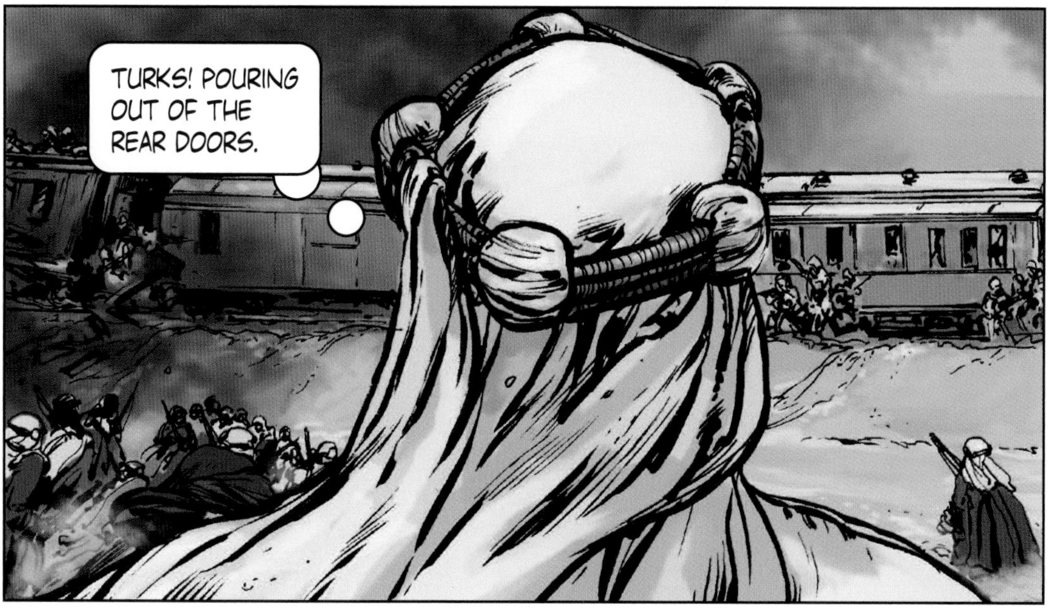
TURKS! POURING OUT OF THE REAR DOORS.

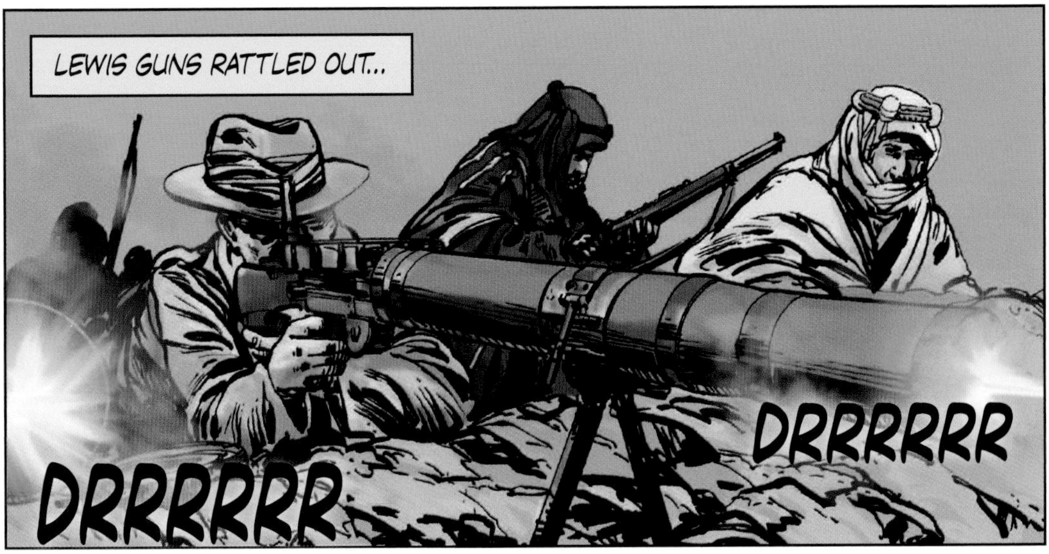
LEWIS GUNS RATTLED OUT...
DRRRRRR
DRRRRRRR

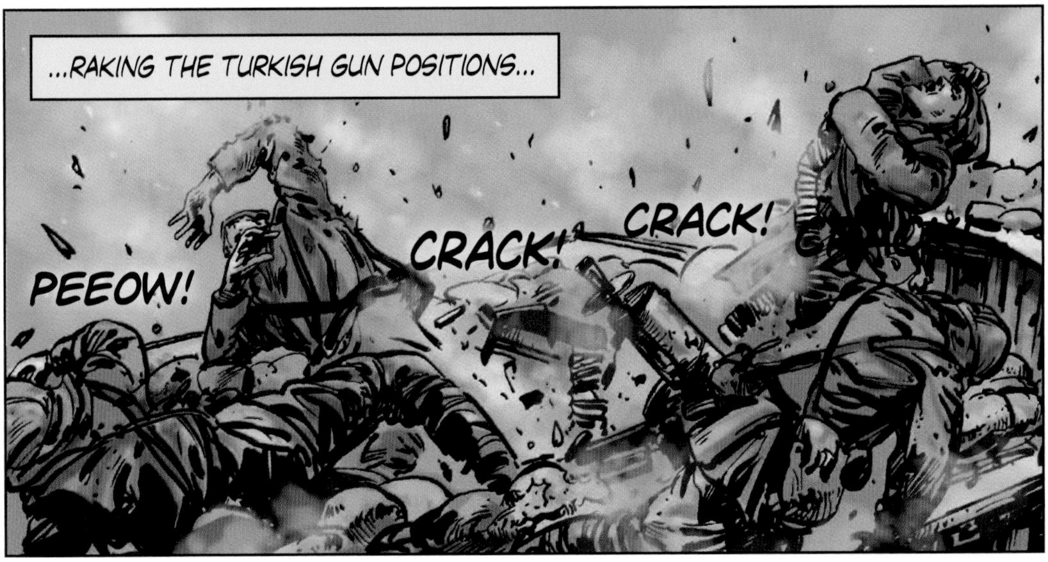
...RAKING THE TURKISH GUN POSITIONS...
PEEOW!
CRACK!
CRACK!

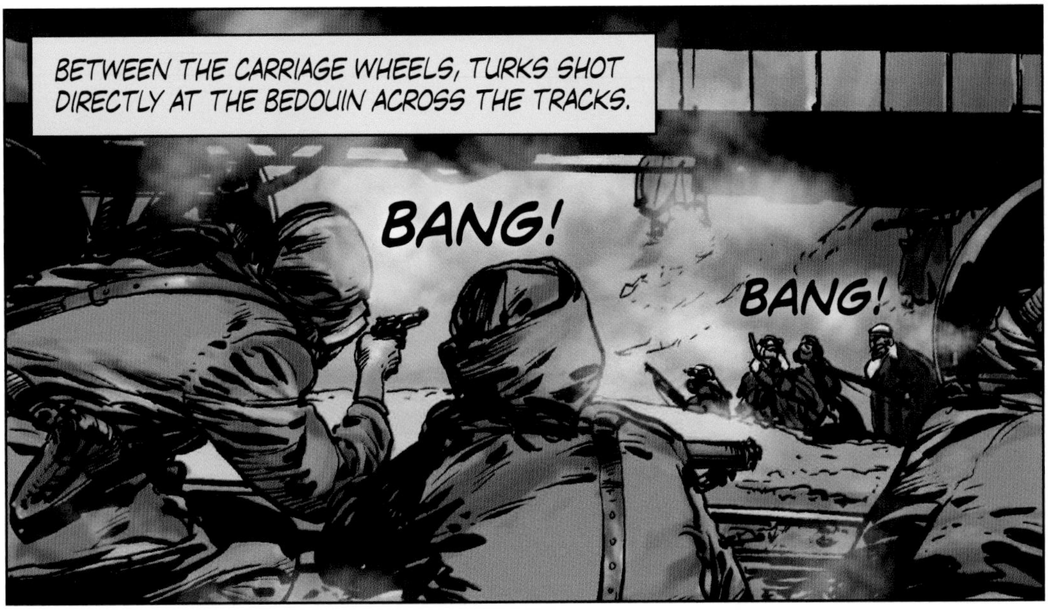
BETWEEN THE CARRIAGE WHEELS, TURKS SHOT DIRECTLY AT THE BEDOUIN ACROSS THE TRACKS.
BANG!
BANG!

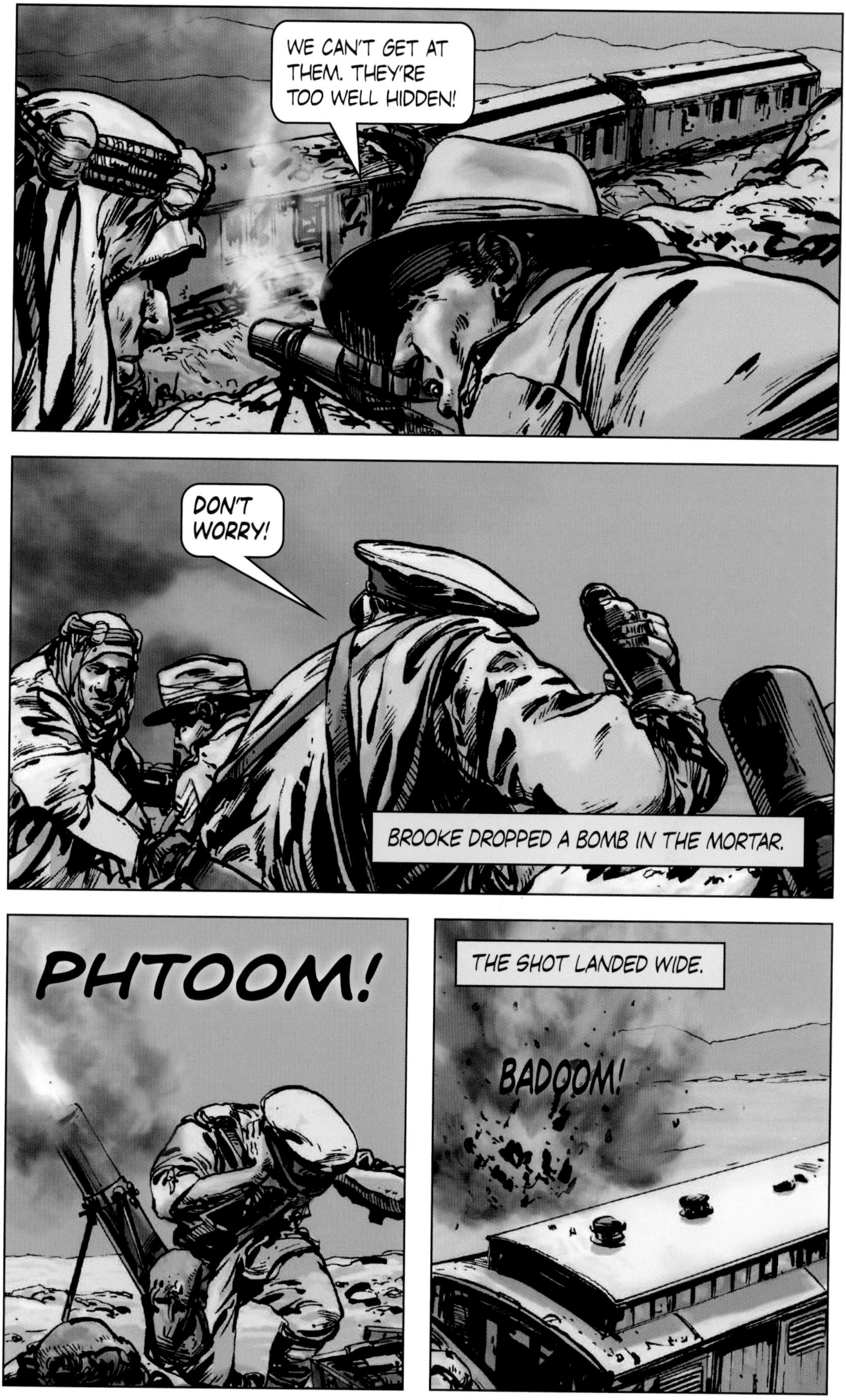
WE CAN'T GET AT THEM. THEY'RE TOO WELL HIDDEN!
DON'T WORRY!
BROOKE DROPPED A BOMB IN THE MORTAR.
PHTOOM!
THE SHOT LANDED WIDE.
BADOOM!

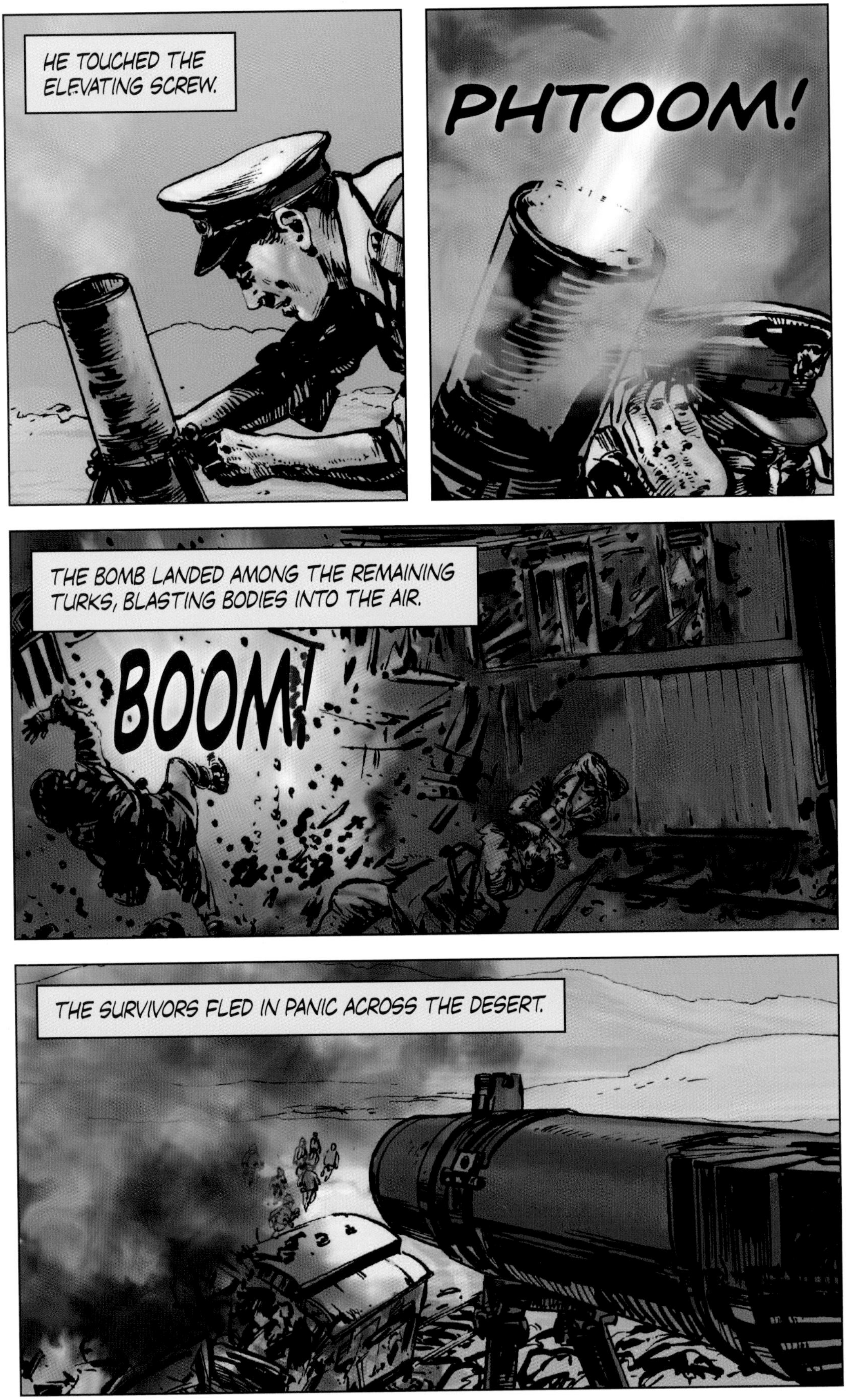
HE TOUCHED THE ELEVATING SCREW.
PHTOOM!
THE BOMB LANDED AMONG THE REMAINING TURKS, BLASTING BODIES INTO THE AIR.
BOOM!
THE SURVIVORS FLED IN PANIC ACROSS THE DESERT.

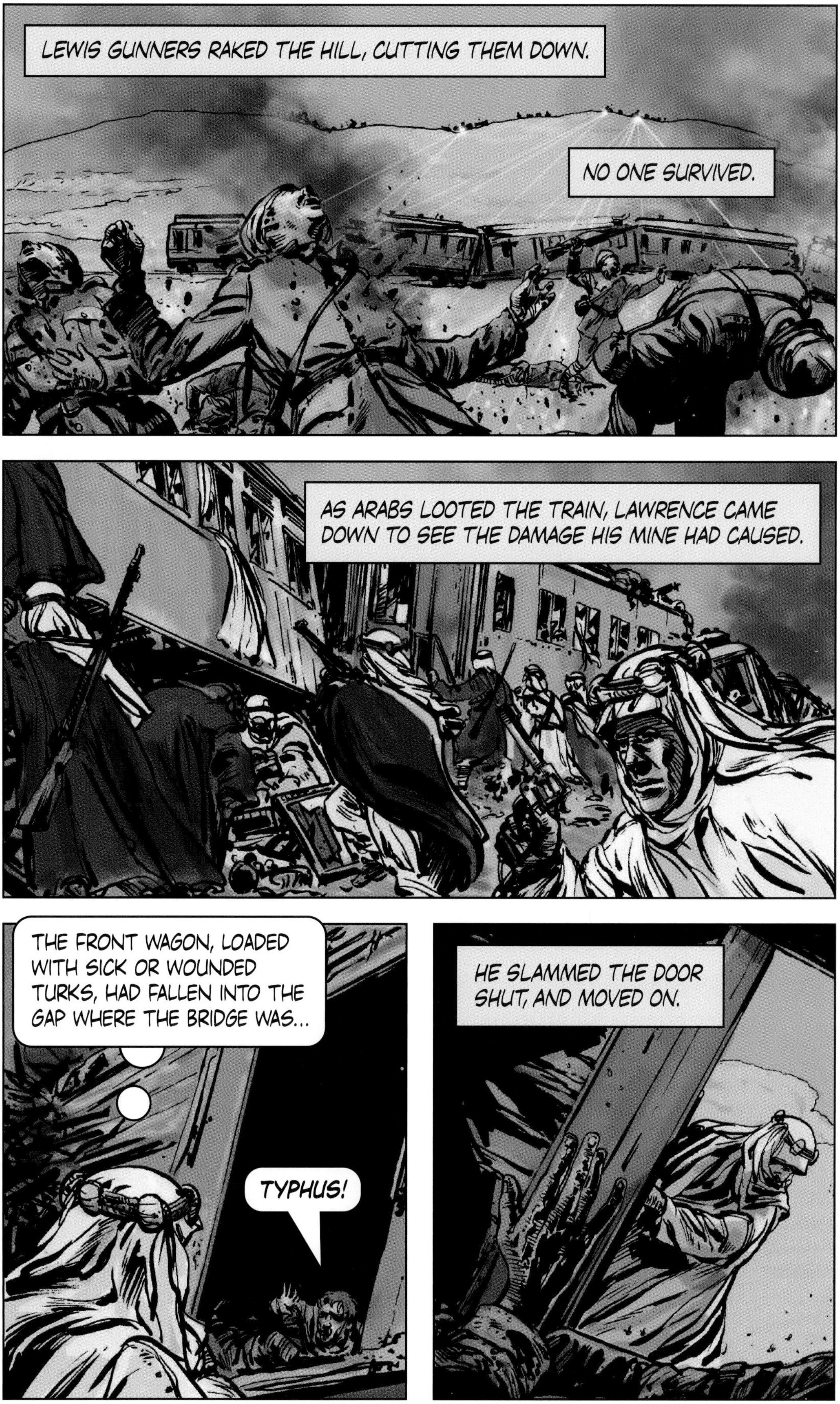
LEWIS GUNNERS RAKED THE HILL, CUTTING THEM DOWN.
NO ONE SURVIVED.
AS ARABS LOOTED THE TRAIN, LAWRENCE CAME DOWN TO SEE THE DAMAGE HIS MINE HAD CAUSED.
THE FRONT WAGON, LOADED WITH SICK OR WOUNDED TURKS, HAD FALLEN INTO THE GAP WHERE THE BRIDGE WAS...
TYPHUS!
HE SLAMMED THE DOOR SHUT, AND MOVED ON.

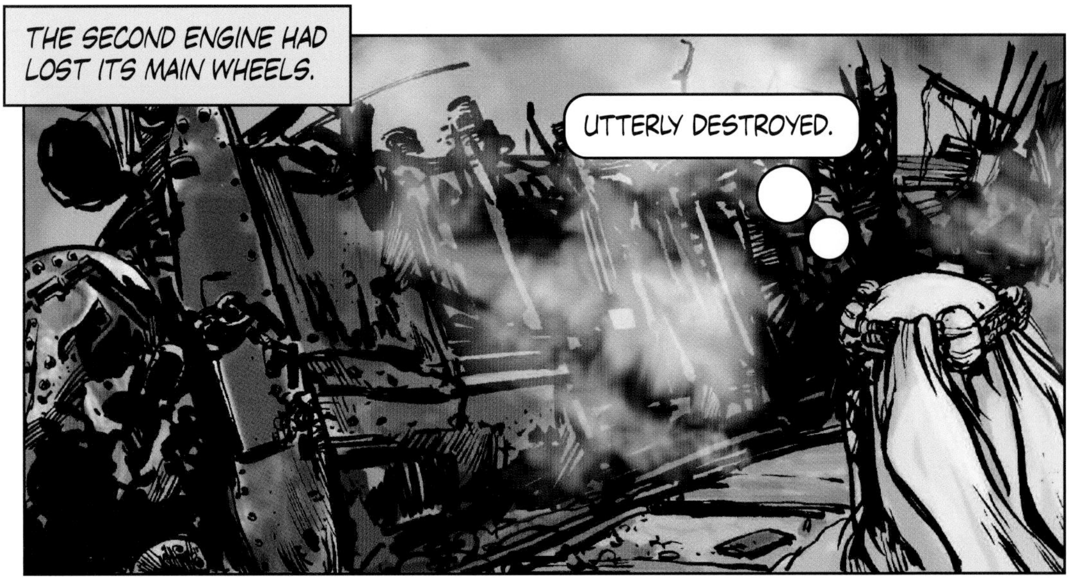
THE SECOND ENGINE HAD LOST ITS MAIN WHEELS.
UTTERLY DESTROYED.

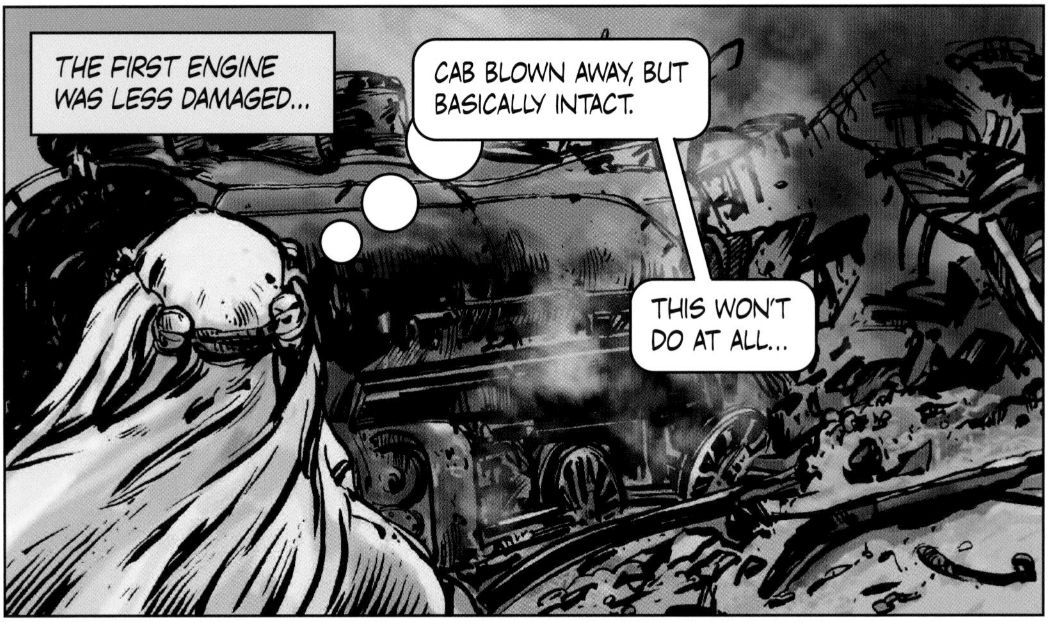
THE FIRST ENGINE WAS LESS DAMAGED...
CAB BLOWN AWAY, BUT BASICALLY INTACT.
THIS WON'T DO AT ALL...

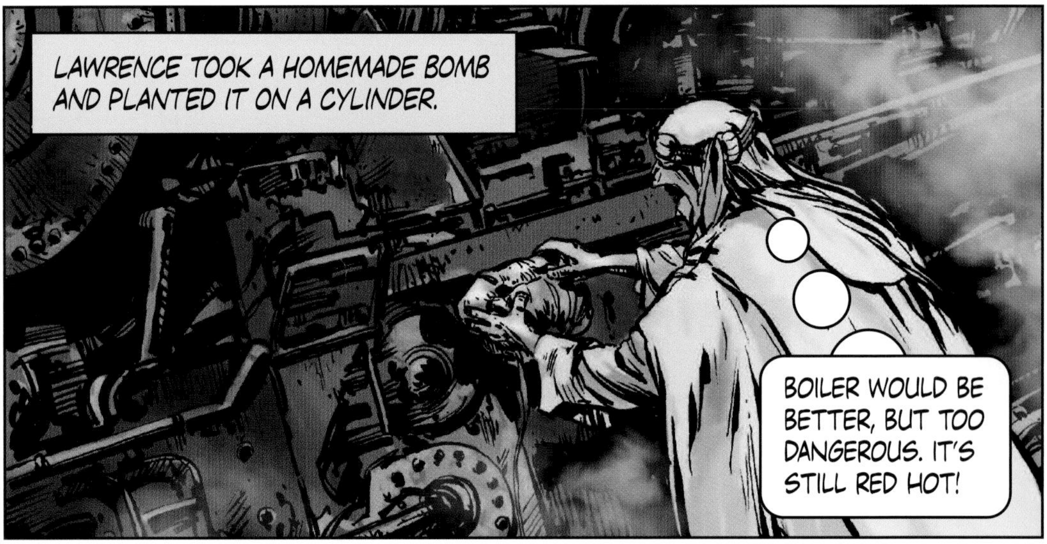
LAWRENCE TOOK A HOMEMADE BOMB AND PLANTED IT ON A CYLINDER.
BOILER WOULD BE BETTER, BUT TOO DANGEROUS. IT'S STILL RED HOT!

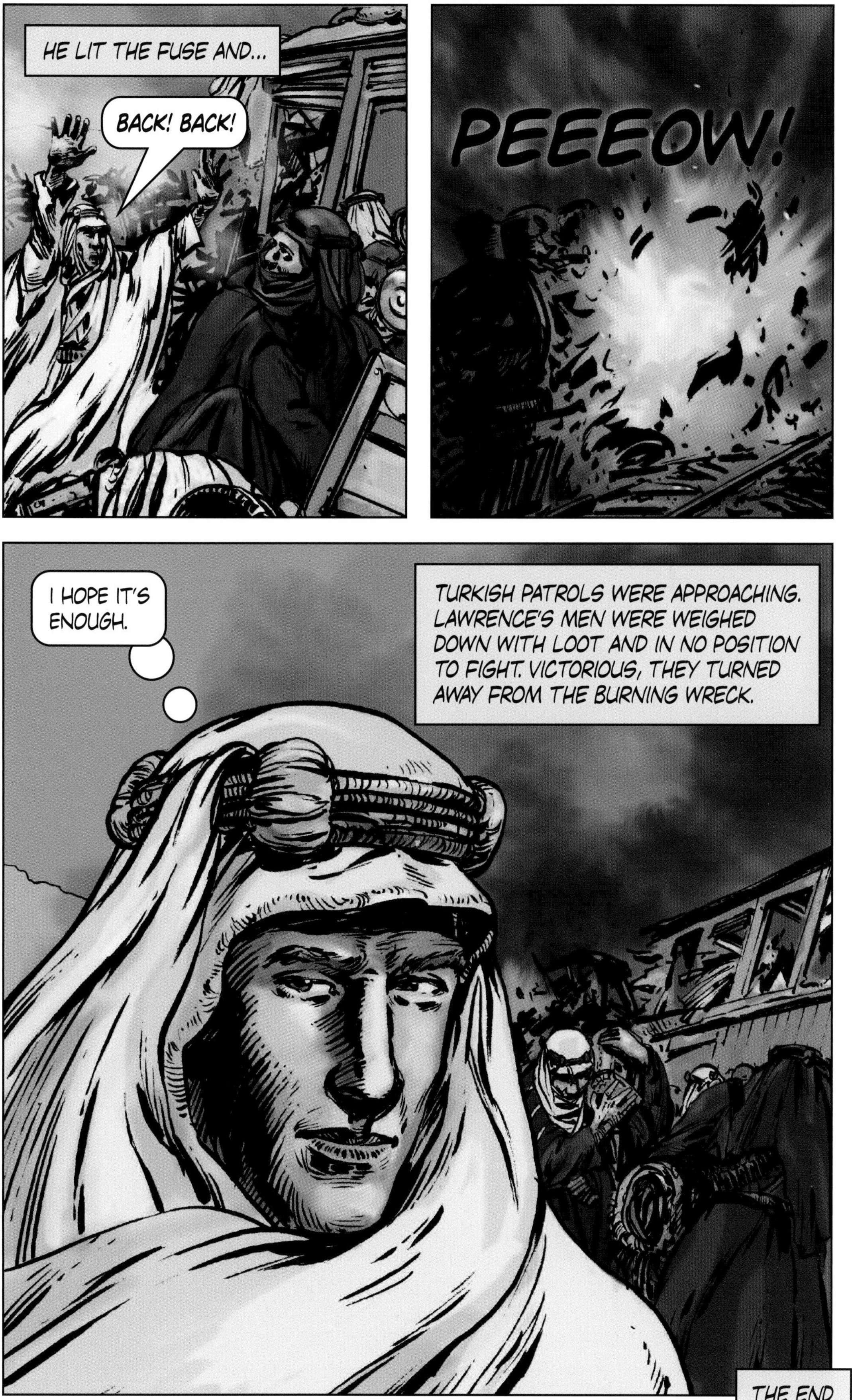
HE LIT THE FUSE AND...
BACK! BACK!
PEEEOW!
I HOPE IT'S ENOUGH.
TURKISH PATROLS WERE APPROACHING. LAWRENCE'S MEN WERE WEIGHED DOWN WITH LOOT AND IN NO POSITION TO FIGHT. VICTORIOUS, THEY TURNED AWAY FROM THE BURNING WRECK.
THE END

THE CHARGE ON BEERSHEBA

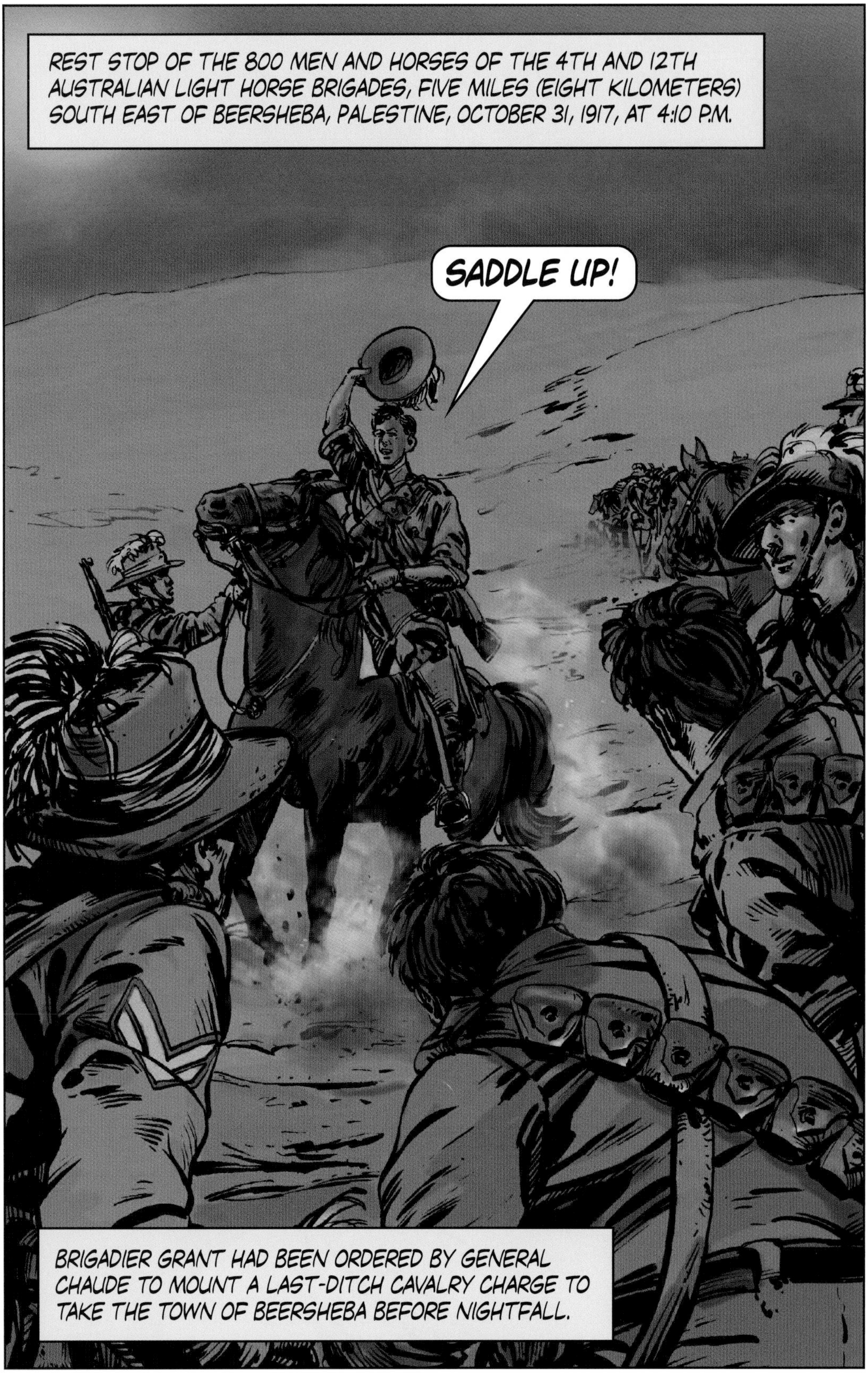
REST STOP OF THE 800 MEN AND HORSES OF THE 4TH AND 12TH AUSTRALIAN LIGHT HORSE BRIGADES, FIVE MILES (EIGHT KILOMETERS) SOUTH EAST OF BEERSHEBA, PALESTINE, OCTOBER 31, 1917, AT 4:10 P.M.
SADDLE UP!
BRIGADIER GRANT HAD BEEN ORDERED BY GENERAL CHAUDE TO MOUNT A LAST-DITCH CAVALRY CHARGE TO TAKE THE TOWN OF BEERSHEBA BEFORE NIGHTFALL.

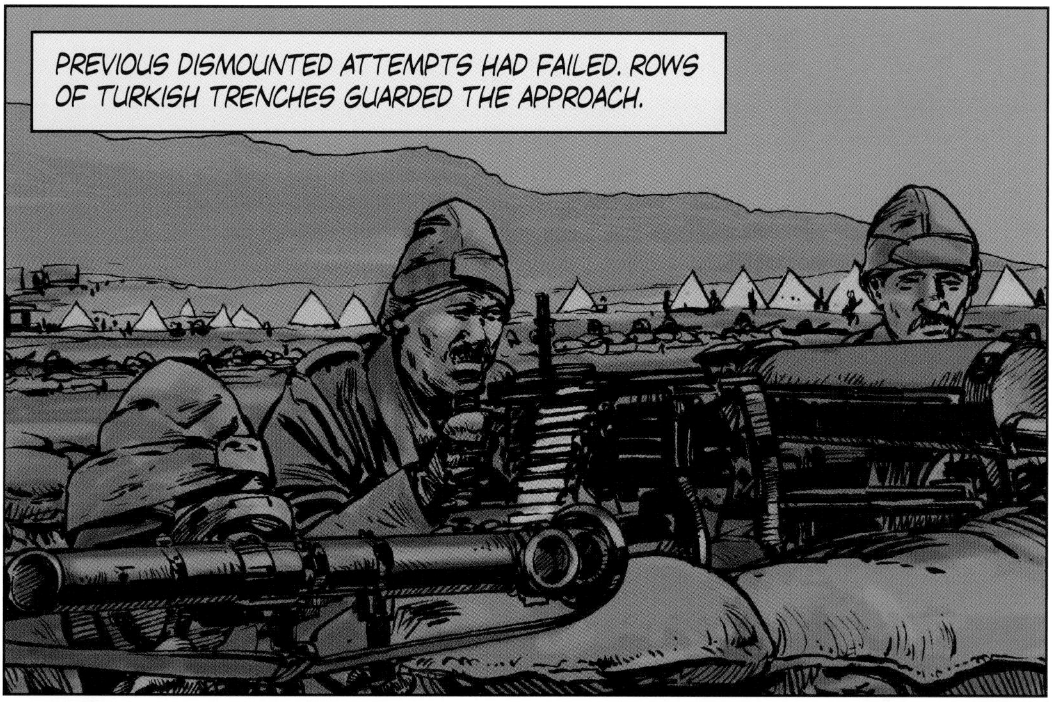
PREVIOUS DISMOUNTED ATTEMPTS HAD FAILED. ROWS OF TURKISH TRENCHES GUARDED THE APPROACH.

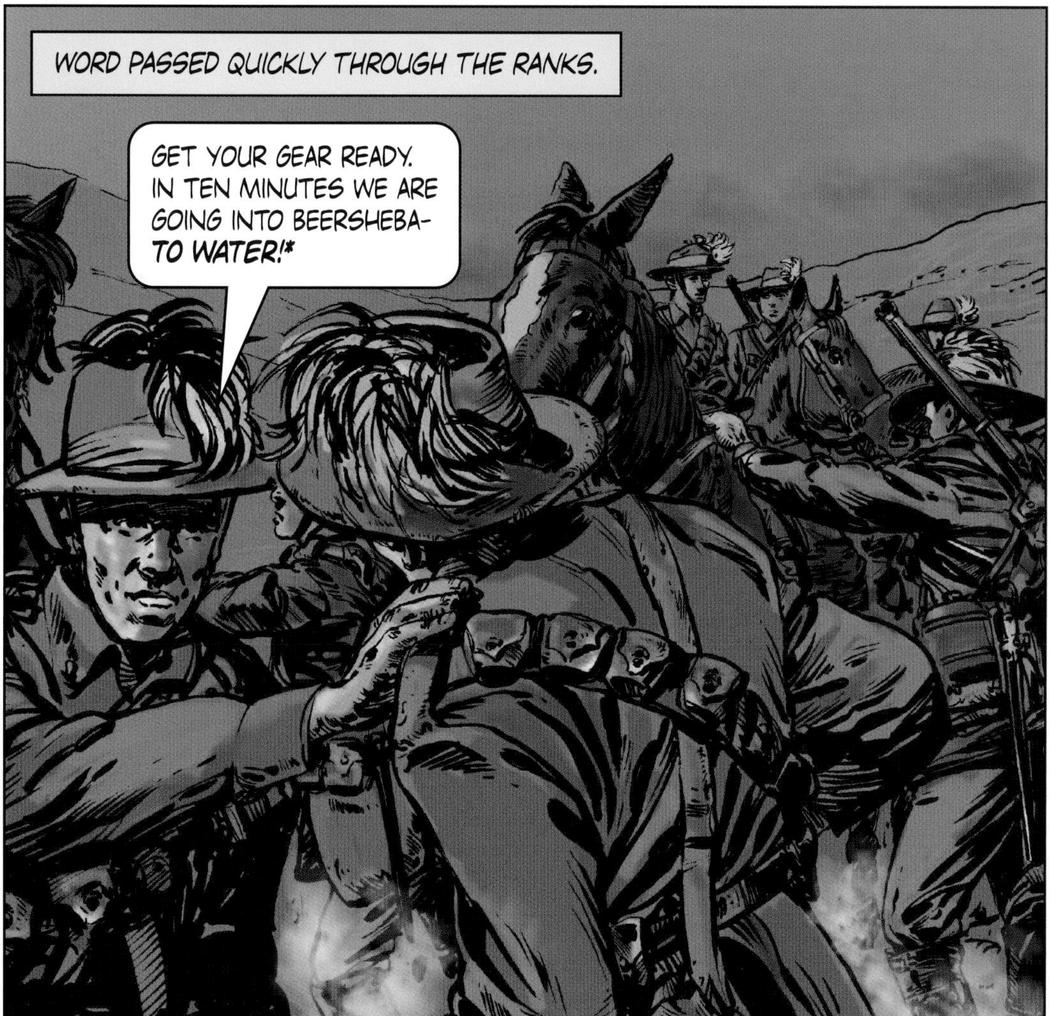
WORD PASSED QUICKLY THROUGH THE RANKS.
GET YOUR GEAR READY. IN TEN MINUTES WE ARE GOING INTO BEERSHEBA- TO WATER!*

*WATER THE HORSES

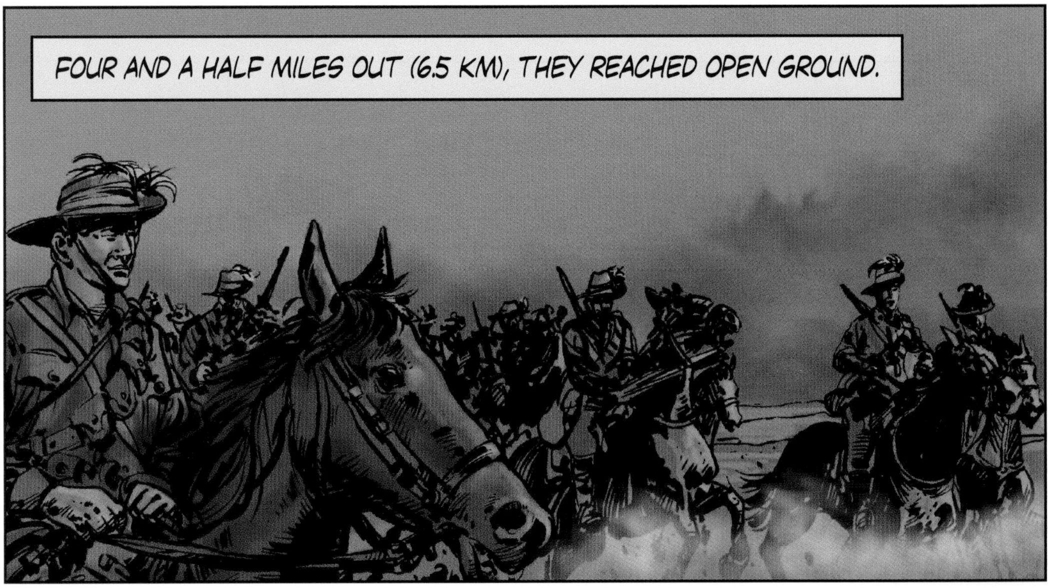
FOUR AND A HALF MILES OUT (6.5 KM), THEY REACHED OPEN GROUND.

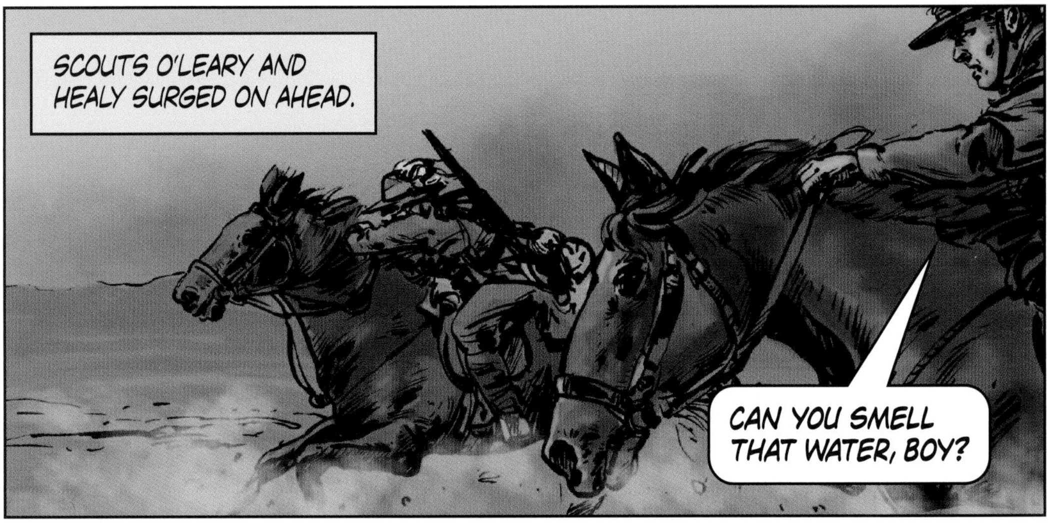
SCOUTS O'LEARY AND HEALY SURGED ON AHEAD.
CAN YOU SMELL THAT WATER, BOY?

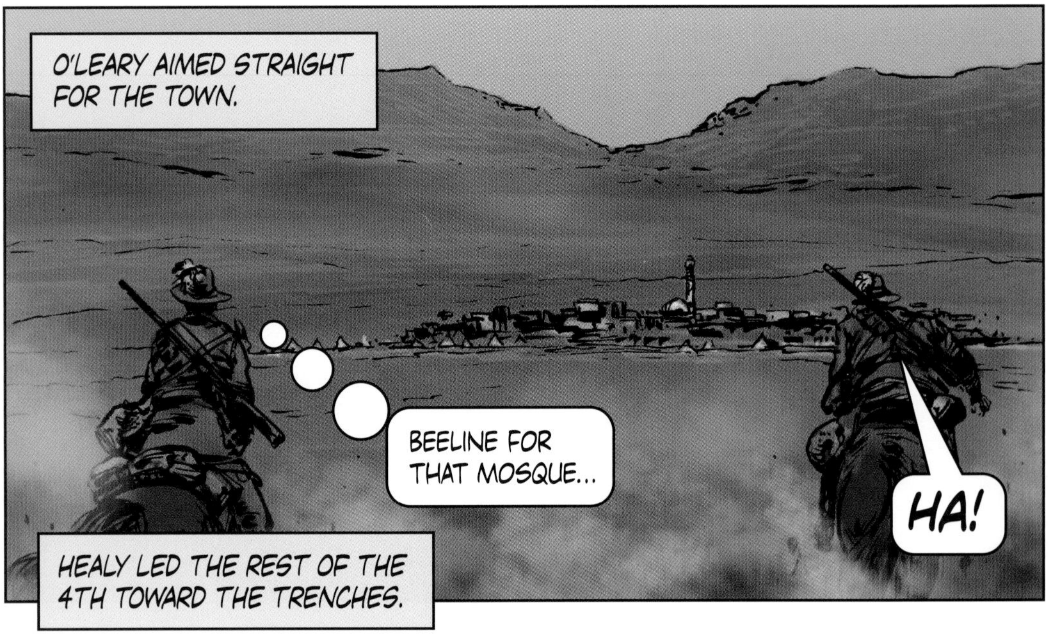
O'LEARY AIMED STRAIGHT FOR THE TOWN.
BEELINE FOR THAT MOSQUE...
HA!
HEALY LED THE REST OF THE 4TH TOWARD THE TRENCHES.

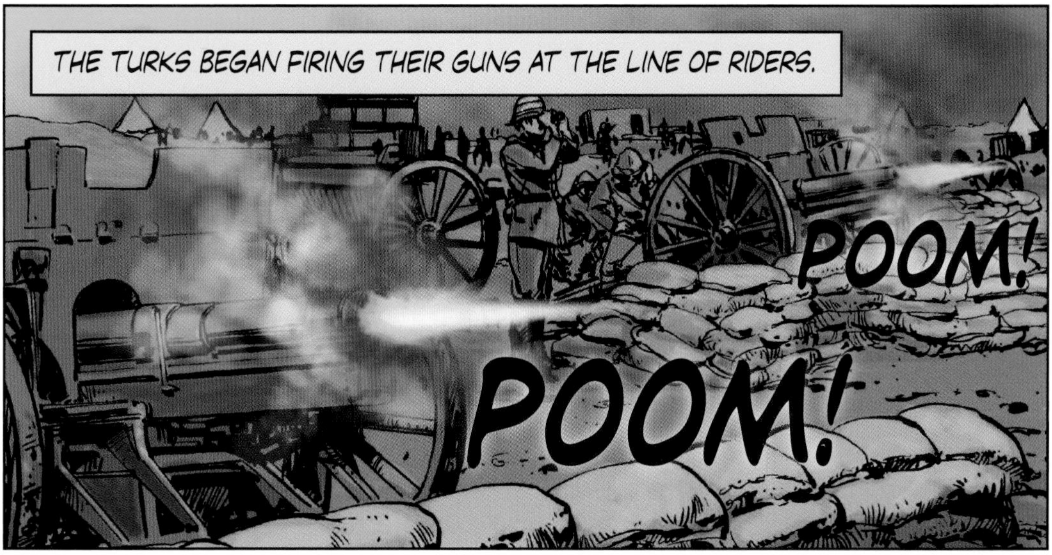
THE TURKS BEGAN FIRING THEIR GUNS AT THE LINE OF RIDERS.
POOM!
POOM!

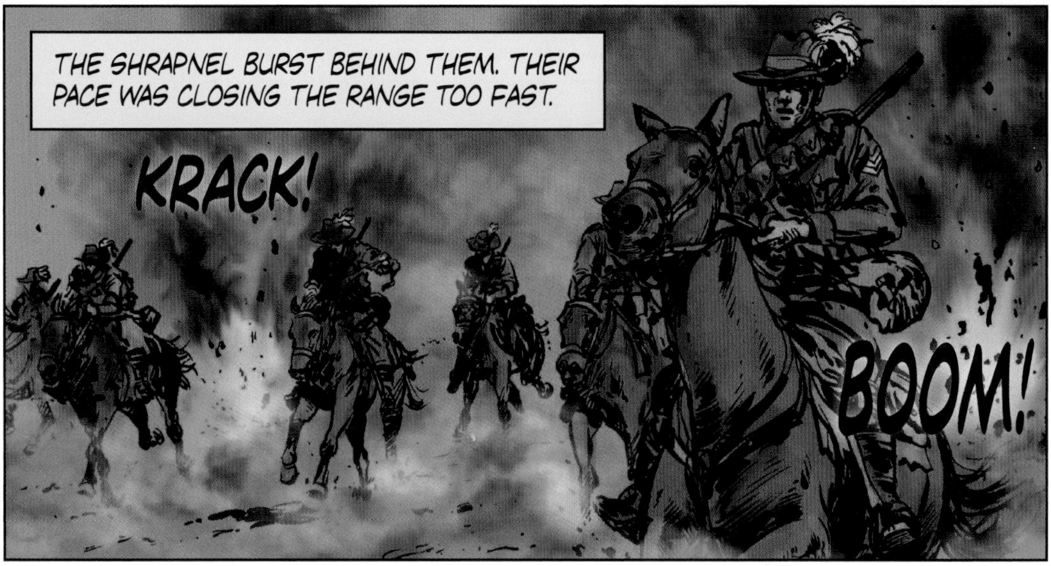
THE SHRAPNEL BURST BEHIND THEM. THEIR PACE WAS CLOSING THE RANGE TOO FAST.
KRACK!
BOOM!

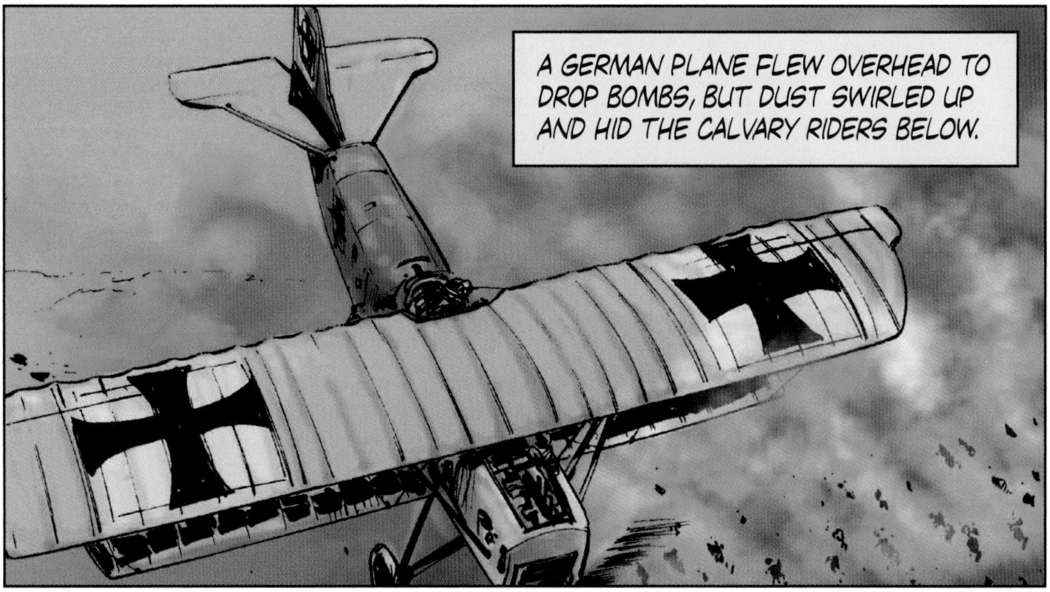
A GERMAN PLANE FLEW OVERHEAD TO DROP BOMBS, BUT DUST SWIRLED UP AND HID THE CALVARY RIDERS BELOW.

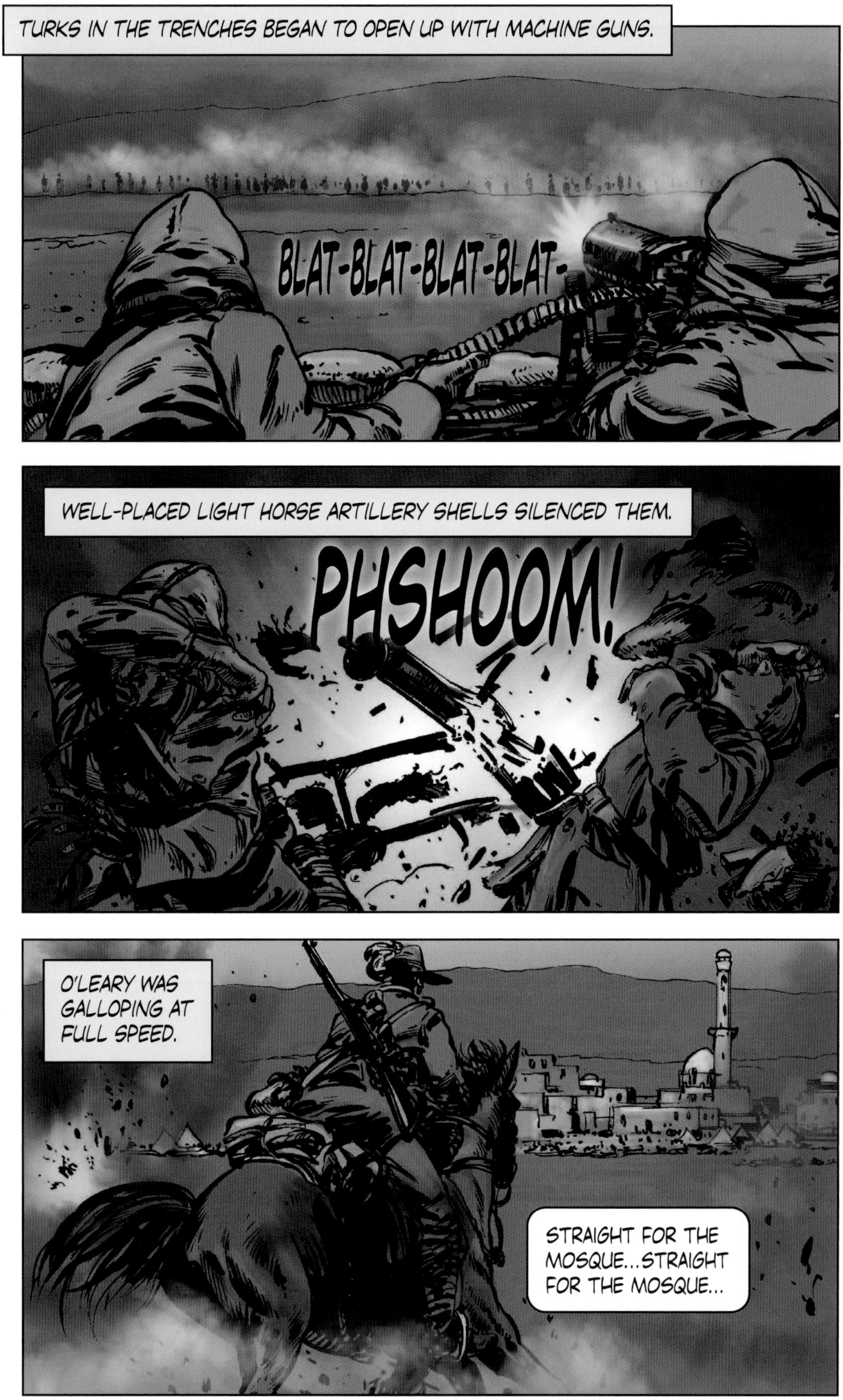
TURKS IN THE TRENCHES BEGAN TO OPEN UP WITH MACHINE GUNS.
BLAT-BLAT-BLAT-BLAT-
WELL-PLACED LIGHT HORSE ARTILLERY SHELLS SILENCED THEM.
PHSHOOM!
O'LEARY WAS GALLOPING AT FULL SPEED.
STRAIGHT FOR THE MOSQUE...STRAIGHT FOR THE MOSQUE...

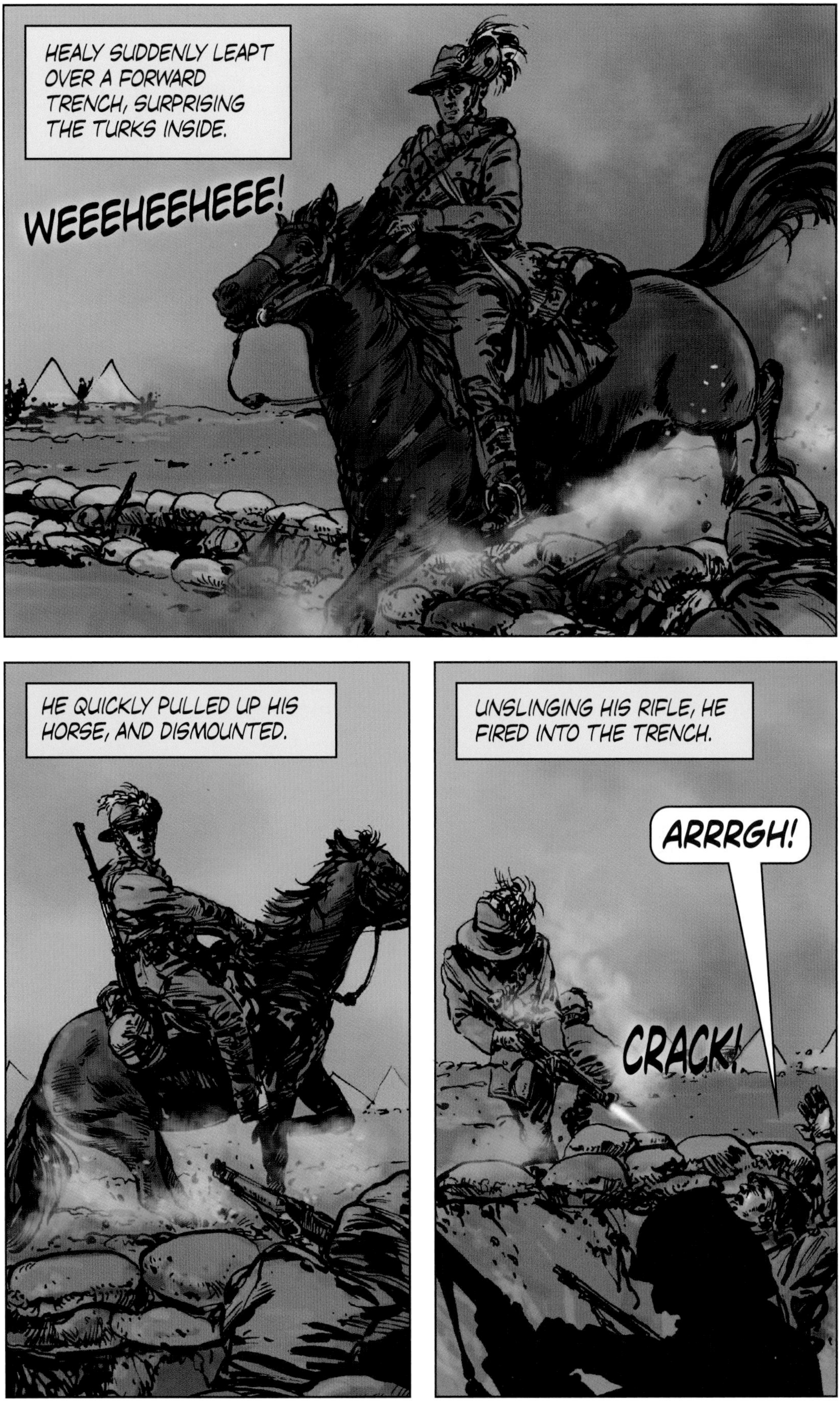
HEALY SUDDENLY LEAPT OVER A FORWARD TRENCH, SURPRISING THE TURKS INSIDE.
WEEEHEEHEEE!
HE QUICKLY PULLED UP HIS HORSE, AND DISMOUNTED.
UNSLINGING HIS RIFLE, HE FIRED INTO THE TRENCH.
ARRRGH!
CRACK!

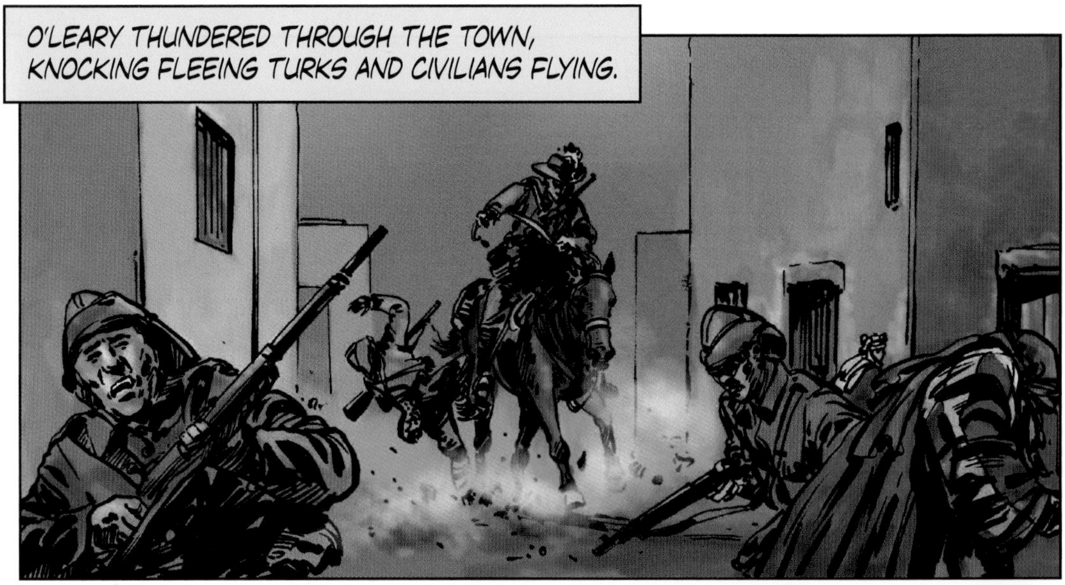
O'LEARY THUNDERED THROUGH THE TOWN, KNOCKING FLEEING TURKS AND CIVILIANS FLYING.

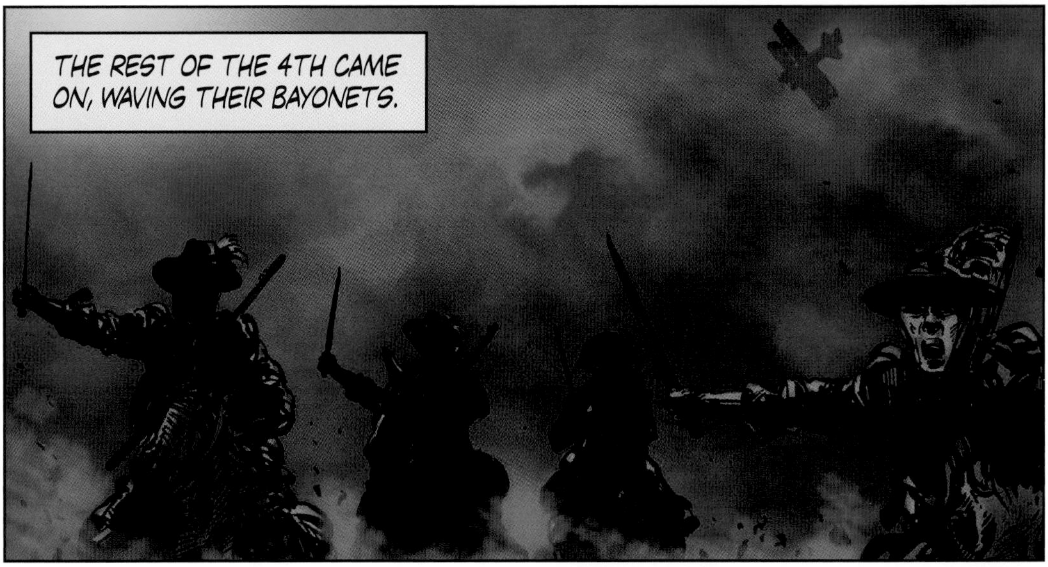
THE REST OF THE 4TH CAME ON, WAVING THEIR BAYONETS.

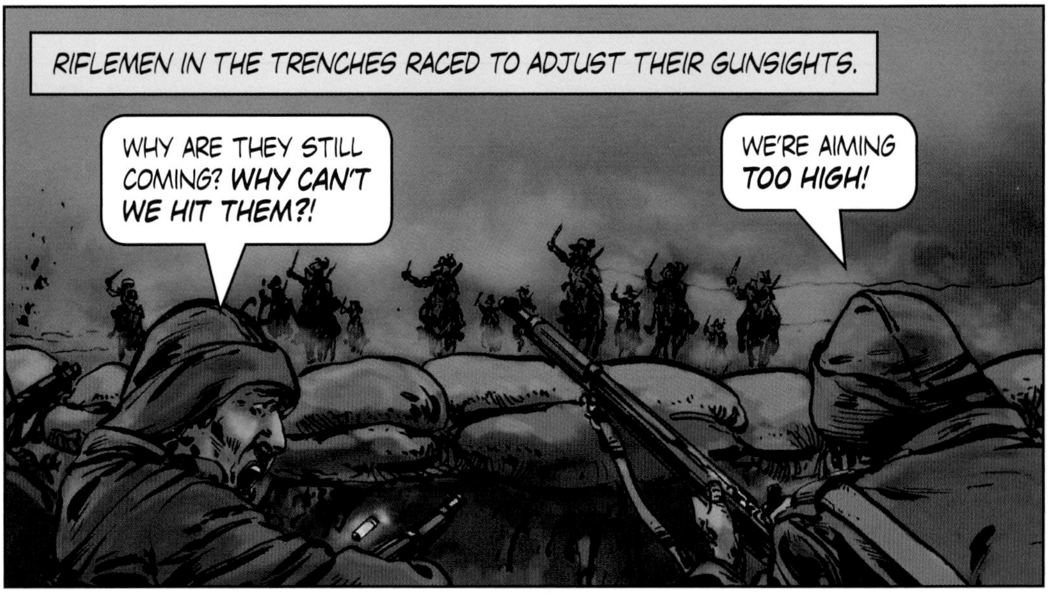
RIFLEMEN IN THE TRENCHES RACED TO ADJUST THEIR GUNSIGHTS.
WHY ARE THEY STILL COMING? WHY CAN'T WE HIT THEM?!
WE'RE AIMING TOO HIGH!

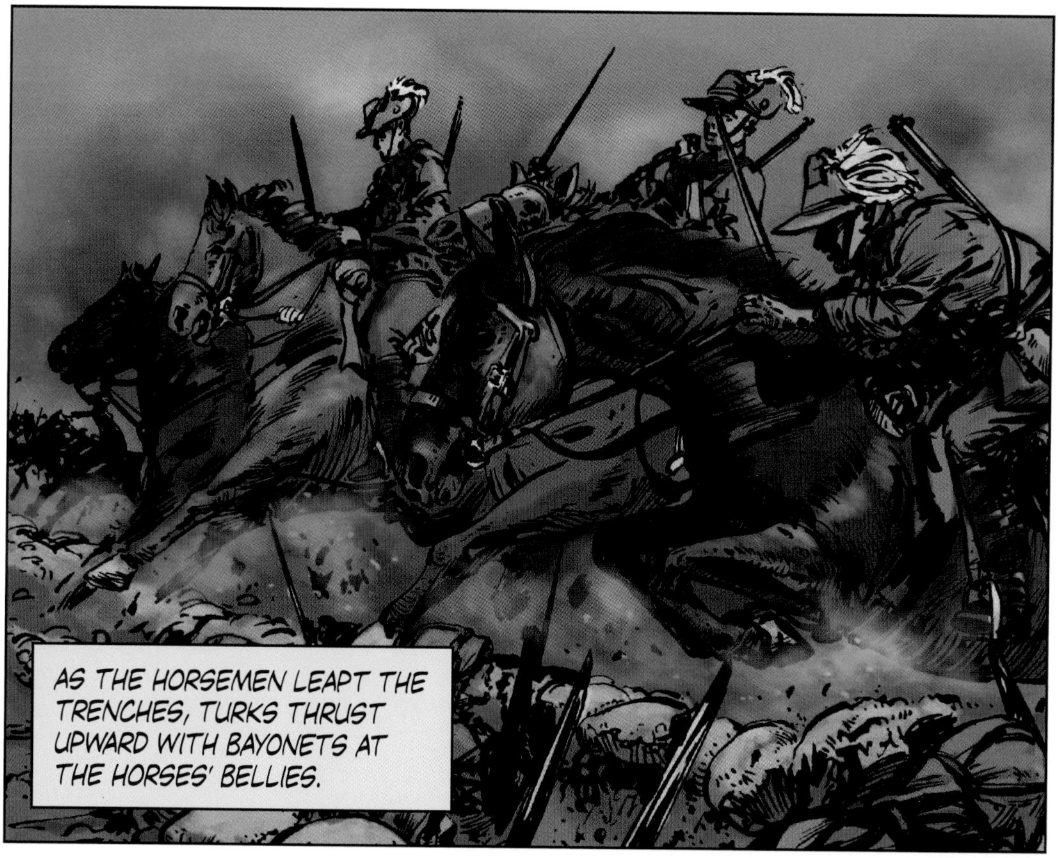
AS THE HORSEMEN LEAPT THE TRENCHES, TURKS THRUST UPWARD WITH BAYONETS AT THE HORSES' BELLIES.

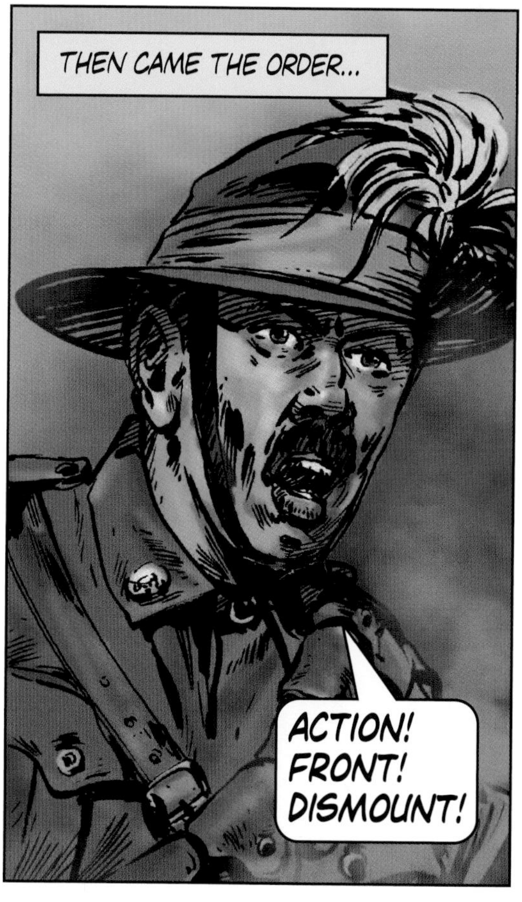
THEN CAME THE ORDER...
ACTION! FRONT! DISMOUNT!

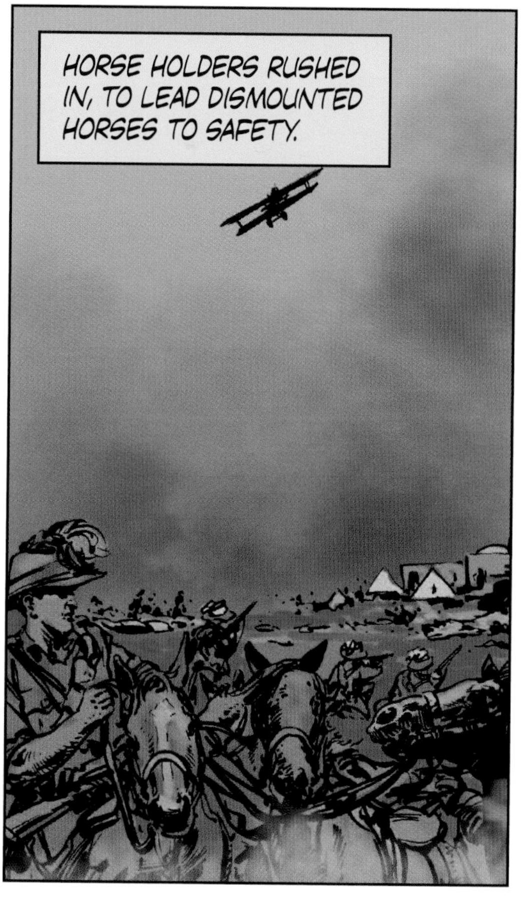
HORSE HOLDERS RUSHED IN, TO LEAD DISMOUNTED HORSES TO SAFETY.

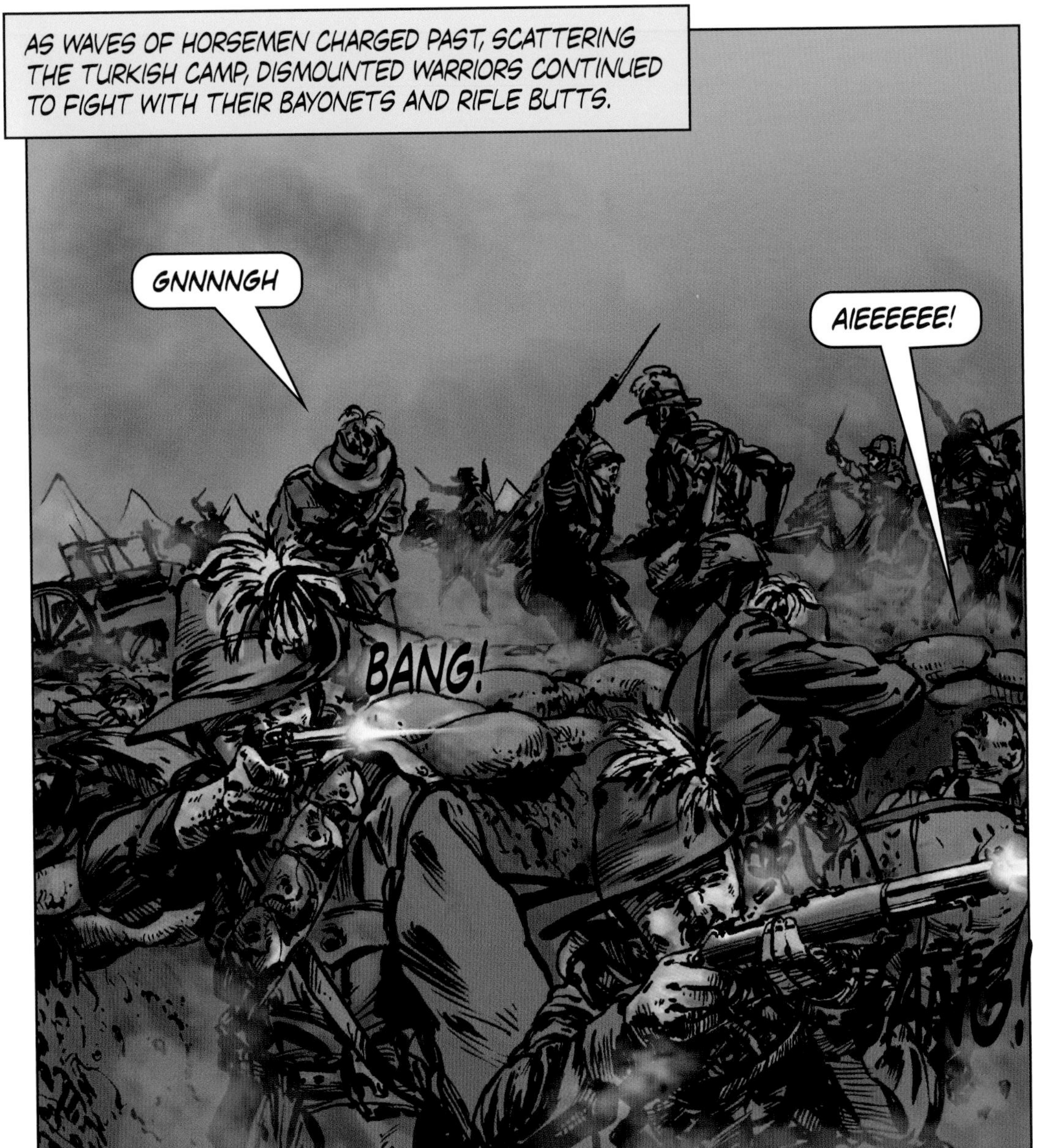
AS WAVES OF HORSEMEN CHARGED PAST, SCATTERING THE TURKISH CAMP, DISMOUNTED WARRIORS CONTINUED TO FIGHT WITH THEIR BAYONETS AND RIFLE BUTTS.
GNNNNGH
AIEEEEEE!
BANG!

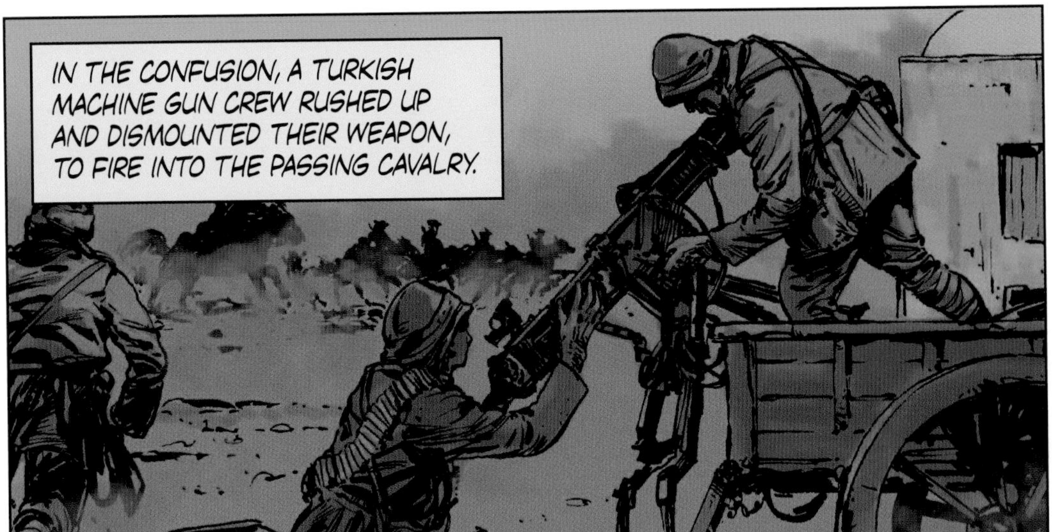
IN THE CONFUSION, A TURKISH MACHINE GUN CREW RUSHED UP AND DISMOUNTED THEIR WEAPON, TO FIRE INTO THE PASSING CAVALRY.

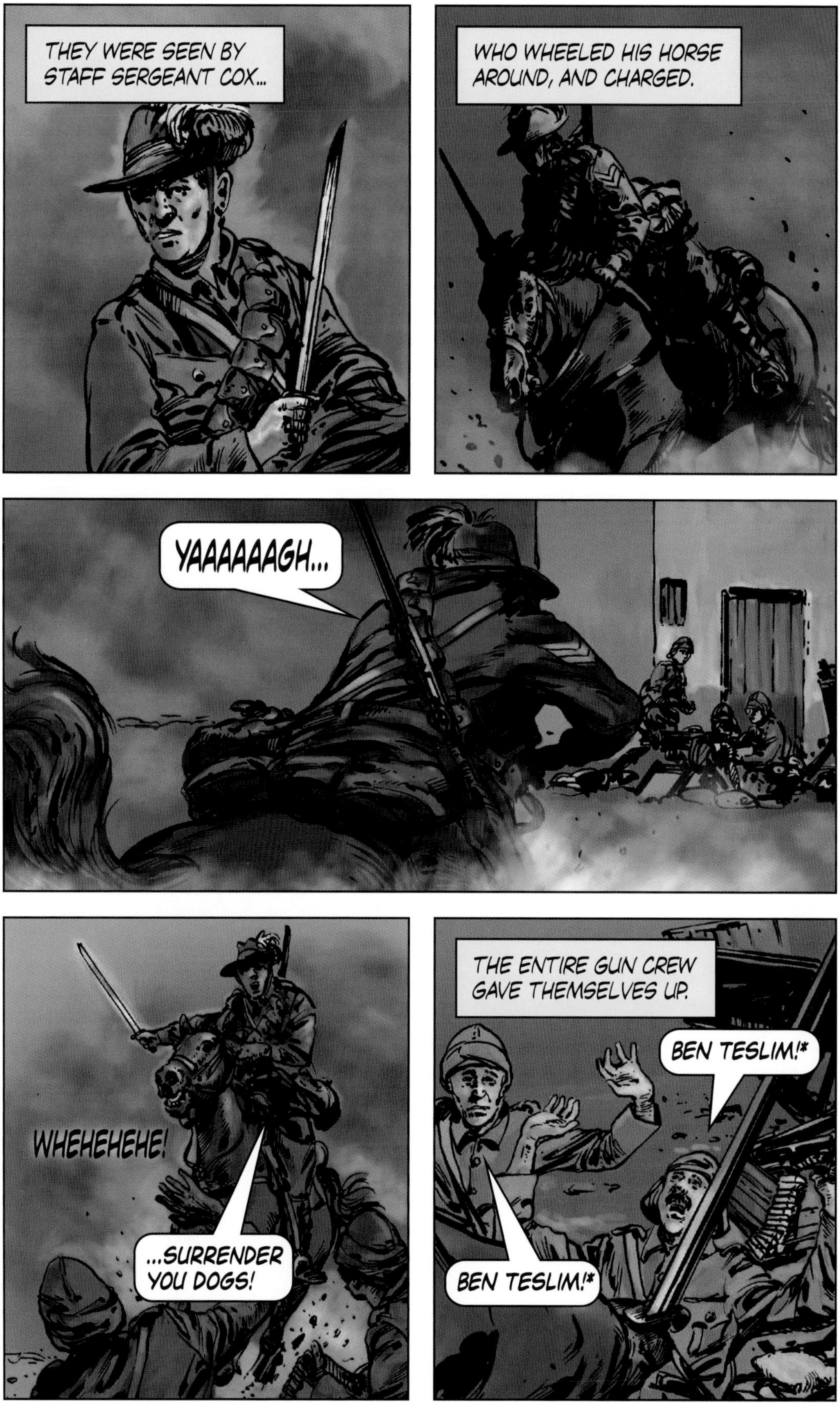
THEY WERE SEEN BY STAFF SERGEANT COX...
WHO WHEELED HIS HORSE AROUND, AND CHARGED.
YAAAAAAGH...
WHEHEHEHE!
...SURRENDER YOU DOGS!
THE ENTIRE GUN CREW GAVE THEMSELVES UP.
BEN TESLIM!*
BEN TESLIM!*

*I SURRENDER

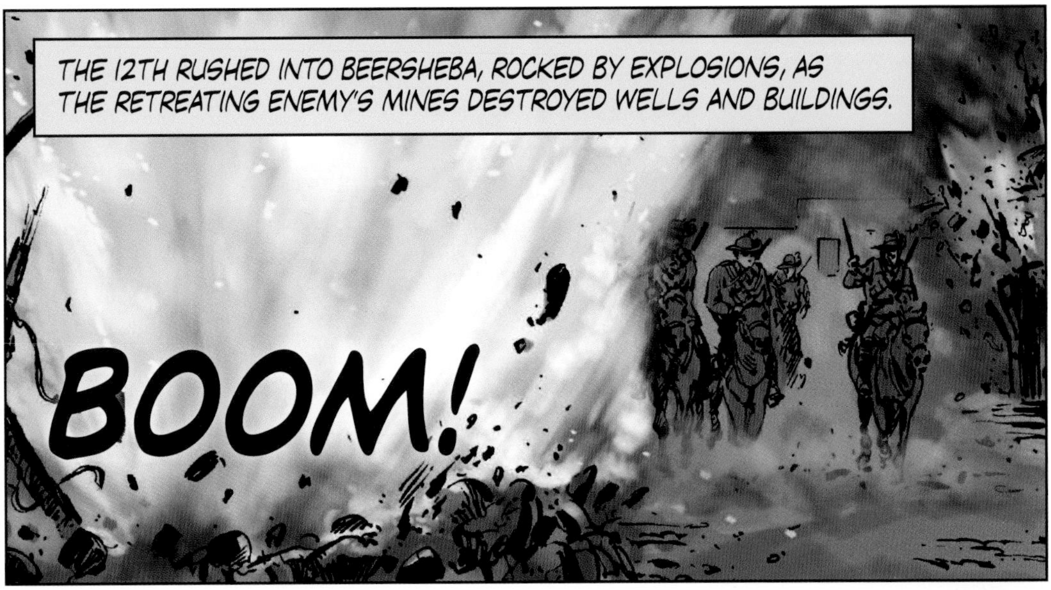
THE 12TH RUSHED INTO BEERSHEBA, ROCKED BY EXPLOSIONS, AS THE RETREATING ENEMY'S MINES DESTROYED WELLS AND BUILDINGS.
BOOM!

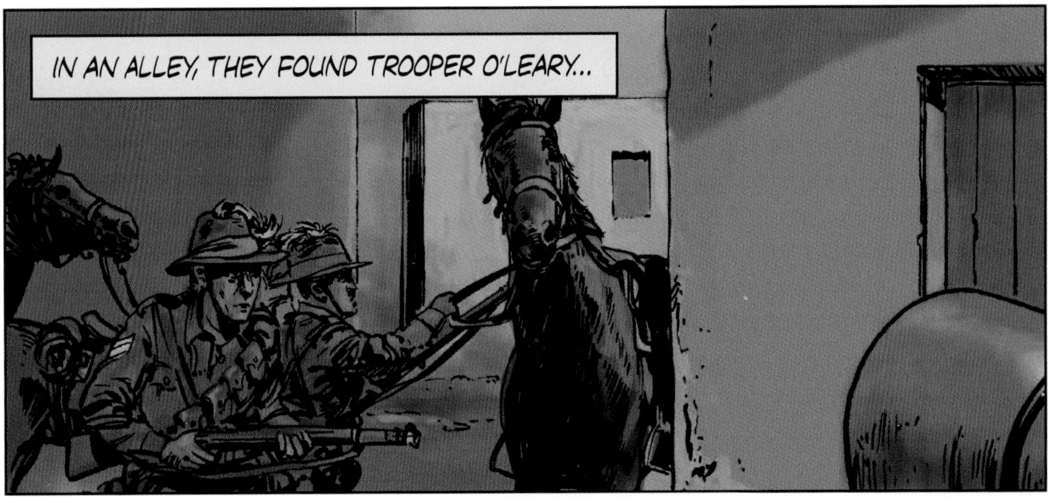
IN AN ALLEY, THEY FOUND TROOPER O'LEARY...

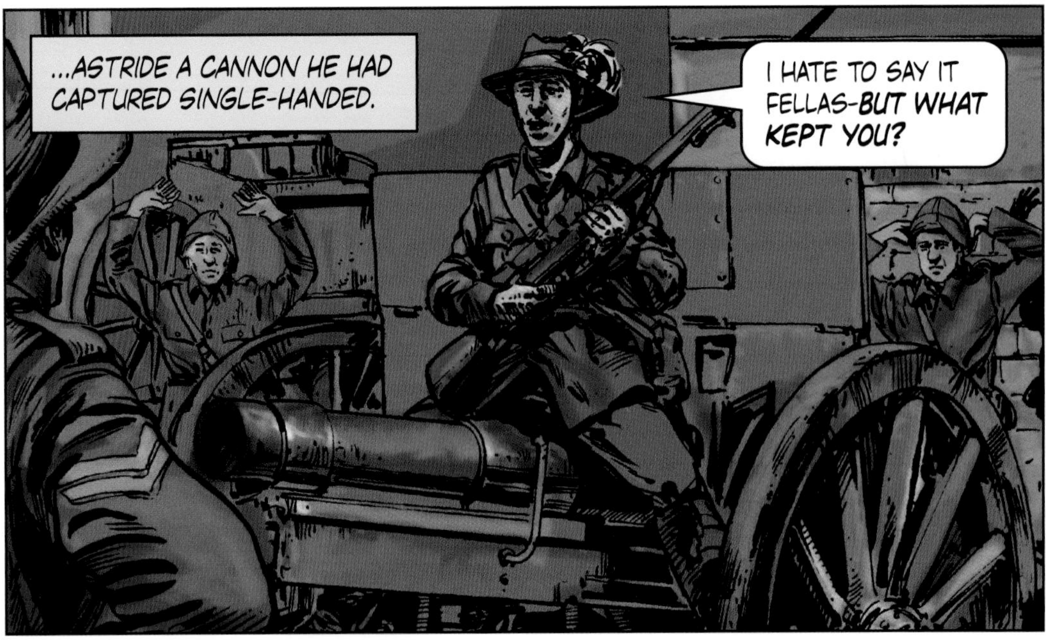
...ASTRIDE A CANNON HE HAD CAPTURED SINGLE-HANDED.
I HATE TO SAY IT FELLAS-BUT WHAT KEPT YOU?

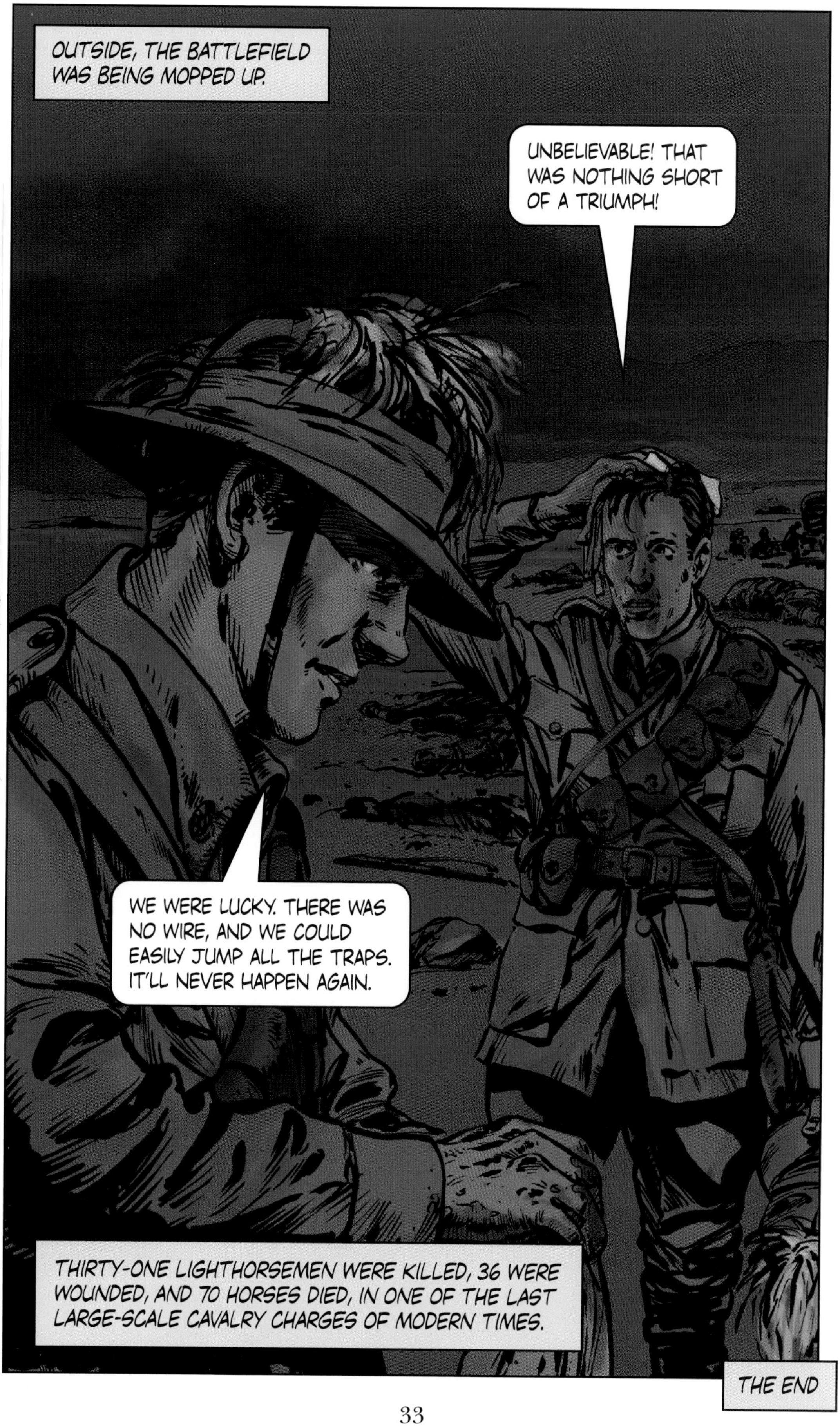
OUTSIDE, THE BATTLEFIELD WAS BEING MOPPED UP.
UNBELIEVABLE! THAT WAS NOTHING SHORT OF A TRIUMPH!
WE WERE LUCKY. THERE WAS NO WIRE, AND WE COULD EASILY JUMP ALL THE TRAPS. IT'LL NEVER HAPPEN AGAIN.
THIRTY-ONE LIGHTHORSEMEN WERE KILLED, 36 WERE WOUNDED, AND 70 HORSES DIED, IN ONE OF THE LAST LARGE-SCALE CAVALRY CHARGES OF MODERN TIMES.
THE END

GALLANTRY AT TEL-EL-SHERIA

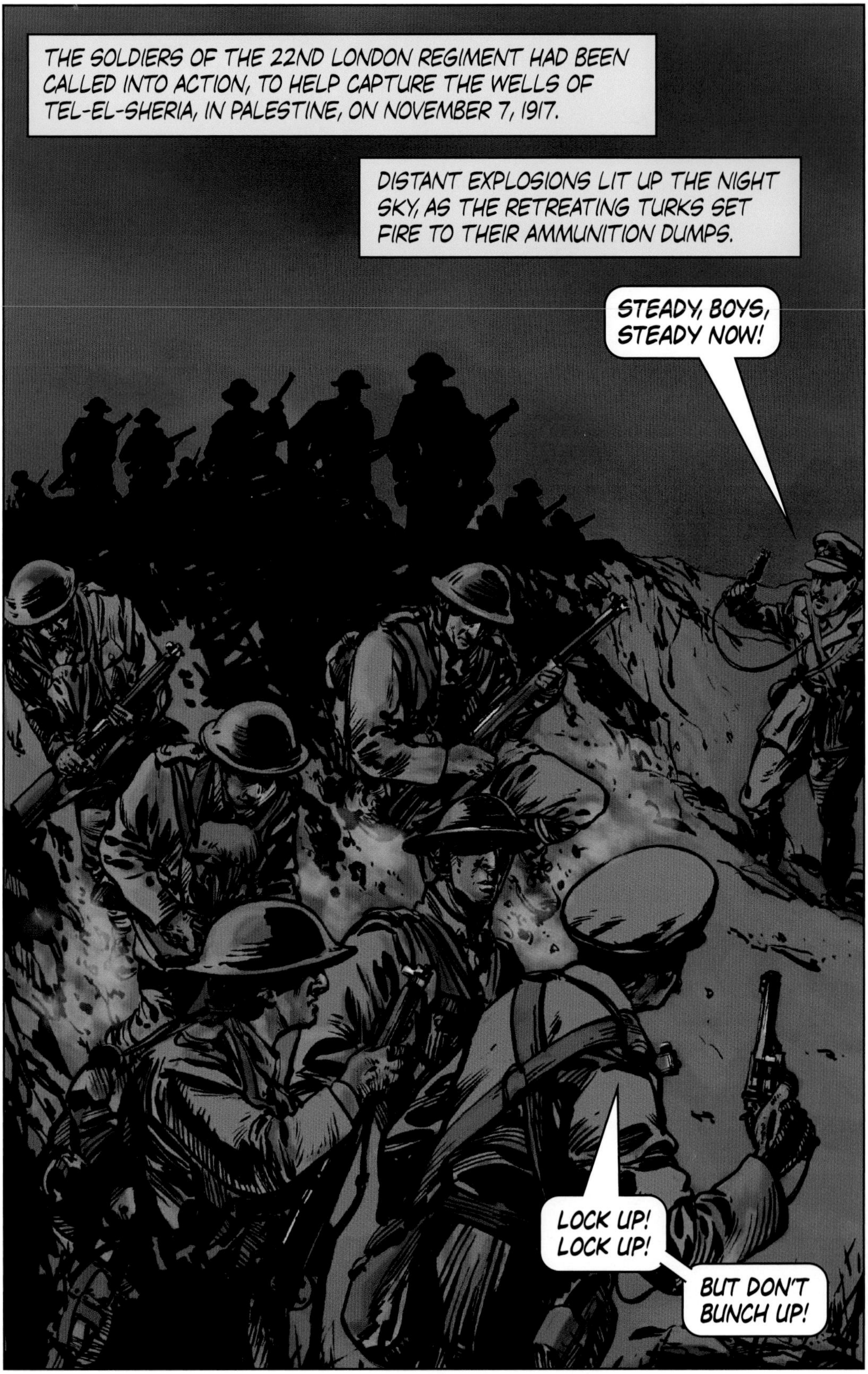

THE SOLDIERS OF THE 22ND LONDON REGIMENT HAD BEEN CALLED INTO ACTION, TO HELP CAPTURE THE WELLS OF TEL-EL-SHERIA, IN PALESTINE, ON NOVEMBER 7, 1917.
DISTANT EXPLOSIONS LIT UP THE NIGHT SKY, AS THE RETREATING TURKS SET FIRE TO THEIR AMMUNITION DUMPS.
STEADY, BOYS, STEADY NOW!
LOCK UP! LOCK UP!
BUT DON'T BUNCH UP!

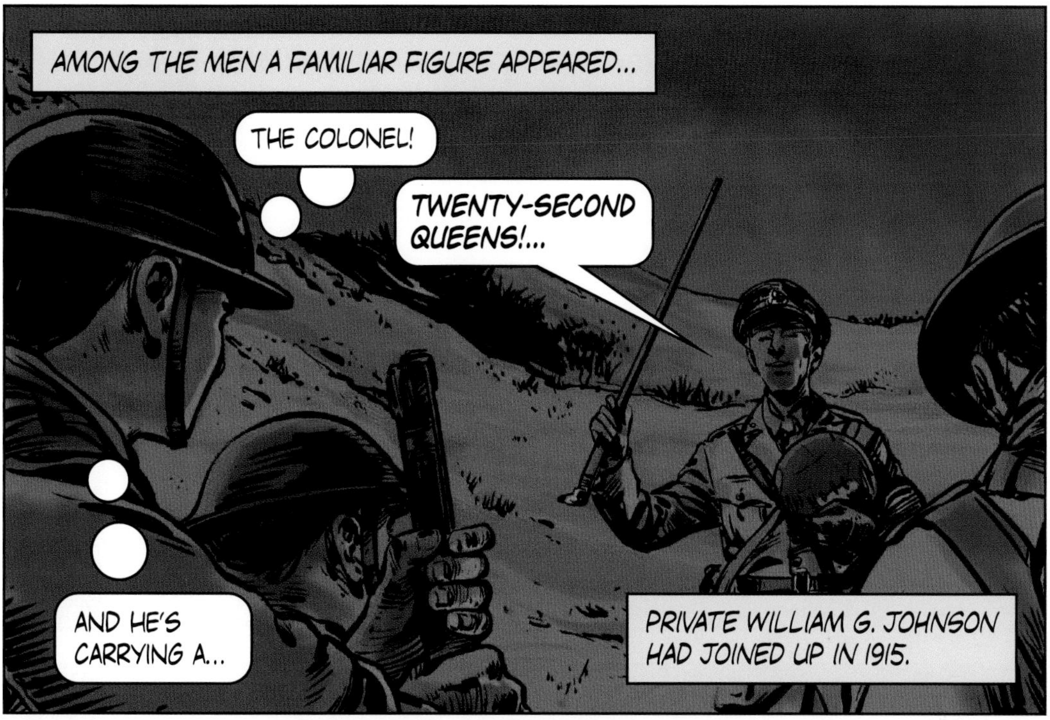
AMONG THE MEN A FAMILIAR FIGURE APPEARED...
THE COLONEL!
TWENTY-SECOND QUEENS!...
AND HE'S CARRYING A...
PRIVATE WILLIAM G. JOHNSON HAD JOINED UP IN 1915.

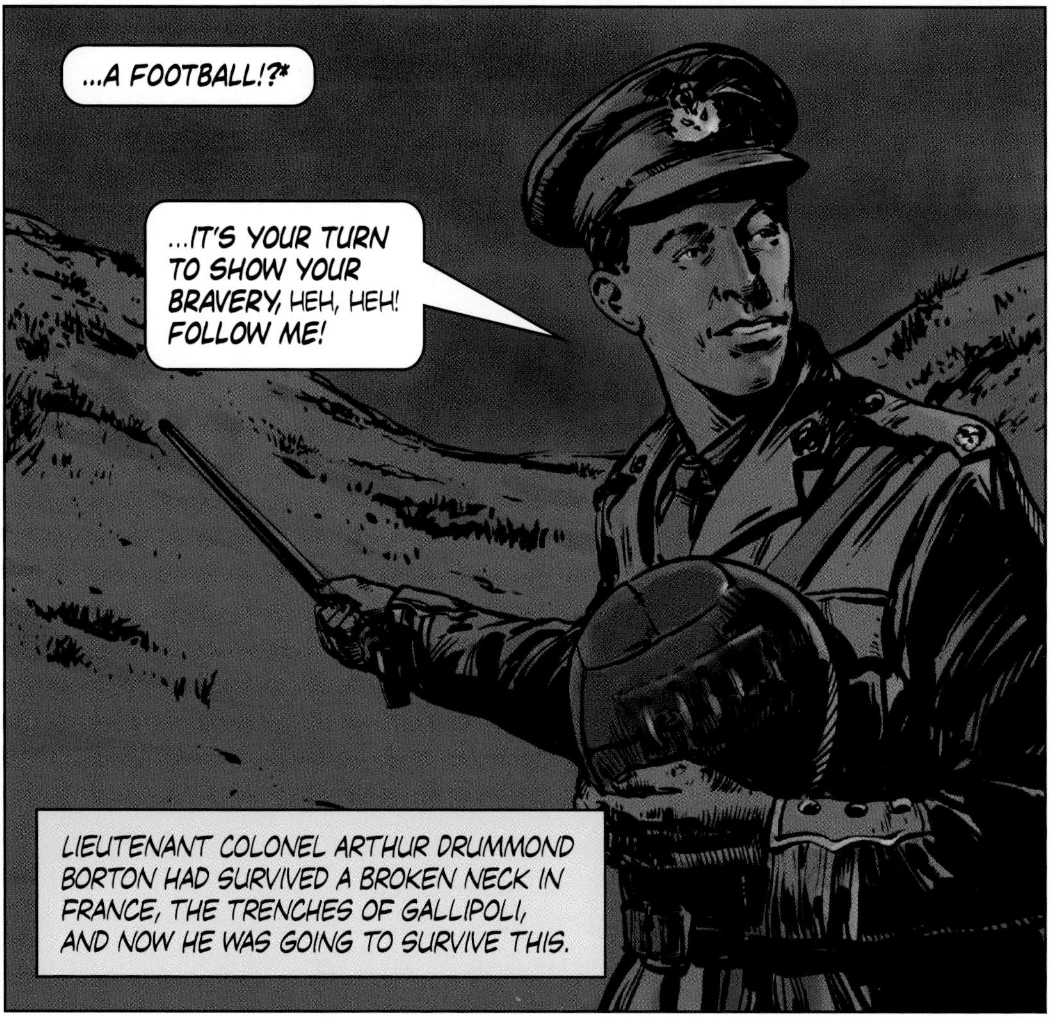
...A FOOTBALL!?*
...IT'S YOUR TURN TO SHOW YOUR BRAVERY, HEH, HEH! FOLLOW ME!
LIEUTENANT COLONEL ARTHUR DRUMMOND BORTON HAD SURVIVED A BROKEN NECK IN FRANCE, THE TRENCHES OF GALLIPOLI, AND NOW HE WAS GOING TO SURVIVE THIS.

*SOCCER BALL

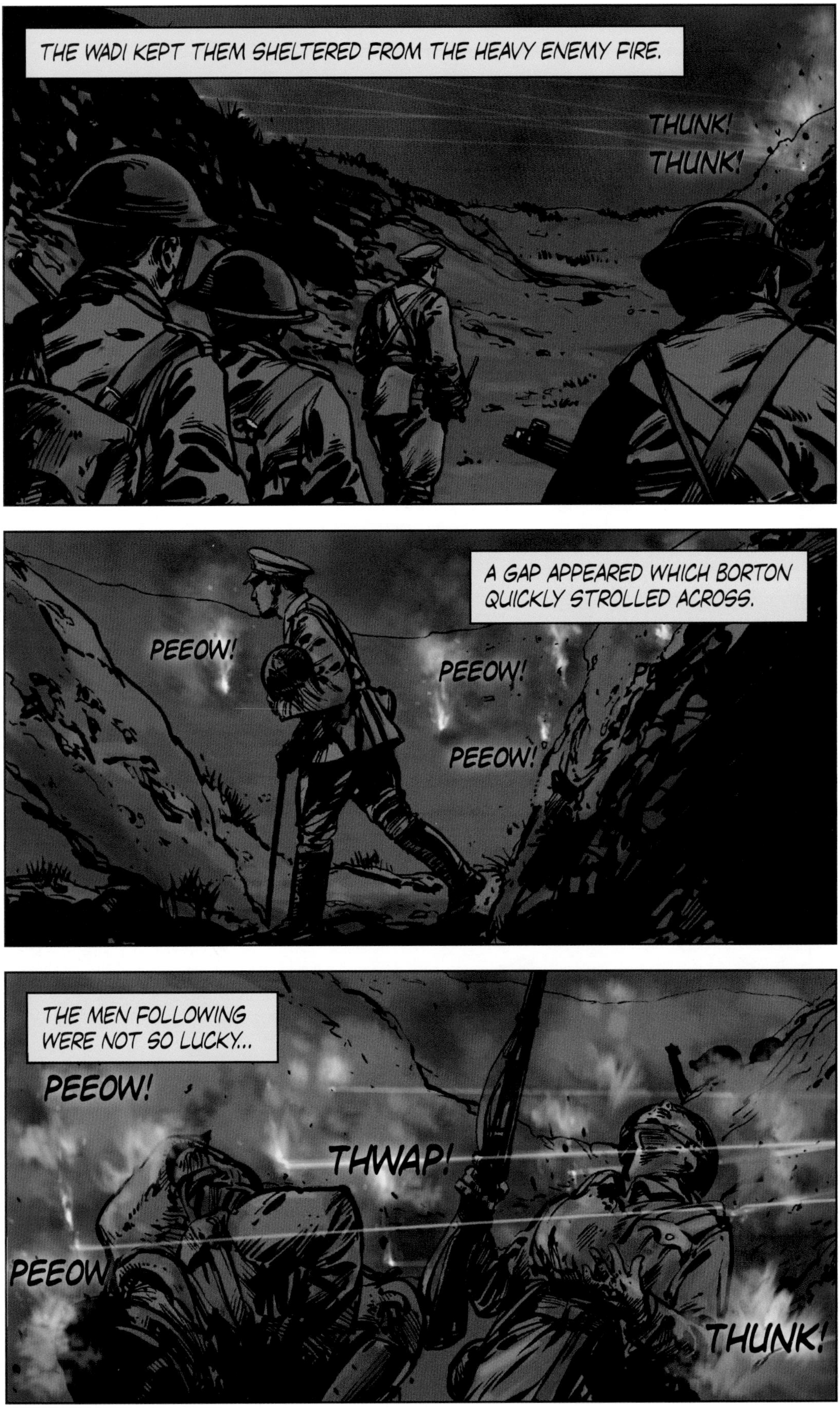
THE WADI KEPT THEM SHELTERED FROM THE HEAVY ENEMY FIRE.
THUNK!
THUNK!
A GAP APPEARED WHICH BORTON QUICKLY STROLLED ACROSS.
PEEOW!
PEEOW!
PEEOW!
THE MEN FOLLOWING WERE NOT SO LUCKY...
PEEOW!
THWAP!
PEEOW
THUNK!

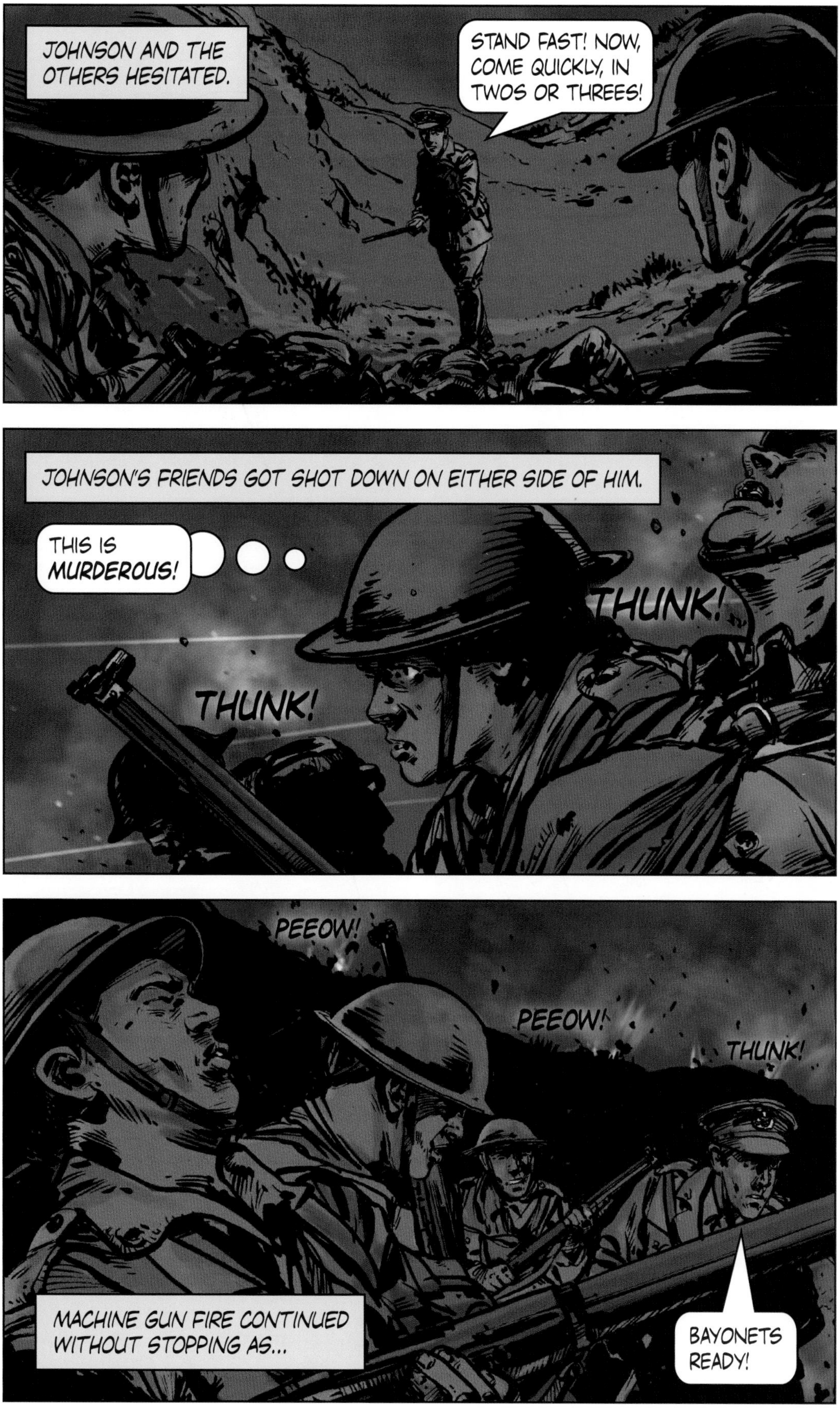
JOHNSON AND THE OTHERS HESITATED.
STAND FAST! NOW, COME QUICKLY, IN TWOS OR THREES!
JOHNSON'S FRIENDS GOT SHOT DOWN ON EITHER SIDE OF HIM.
THIS IS MURDEROUS!
THUNK!
THUNK!
PEEOW!
PEEOW!
THUNK!
MACHINE GUN FIRE CONTINUED WITHOUT STOPPING AS...
BAYONETS READY!

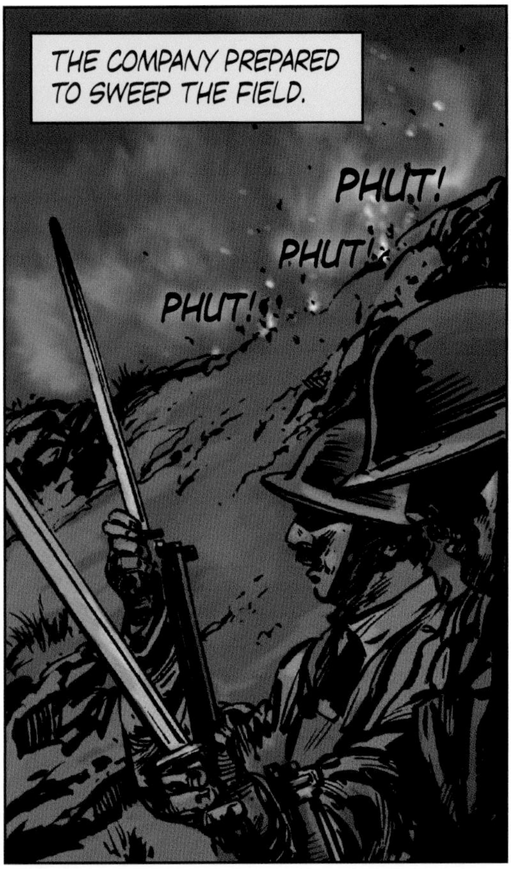
THE COMPANY PREPARED TO SWEEP THE FIELD.
PHUT!
PHUT!
PHUT!

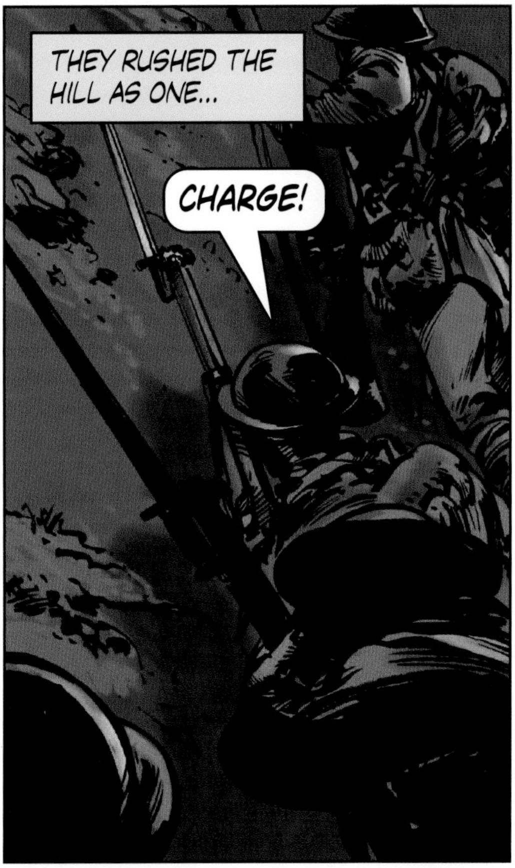
THEY RUSHED THE HILL AS ONE...
CHARGE!

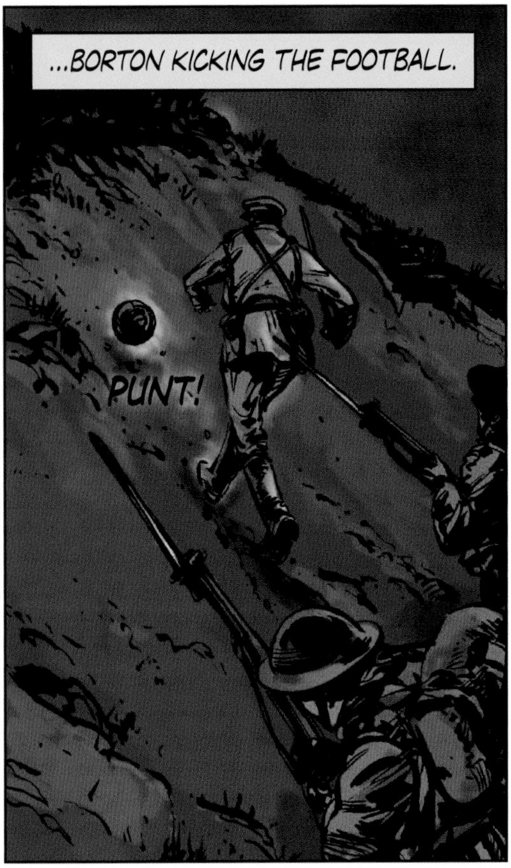
...BORTON KICKING THE FOOTBALL.
PUNT!

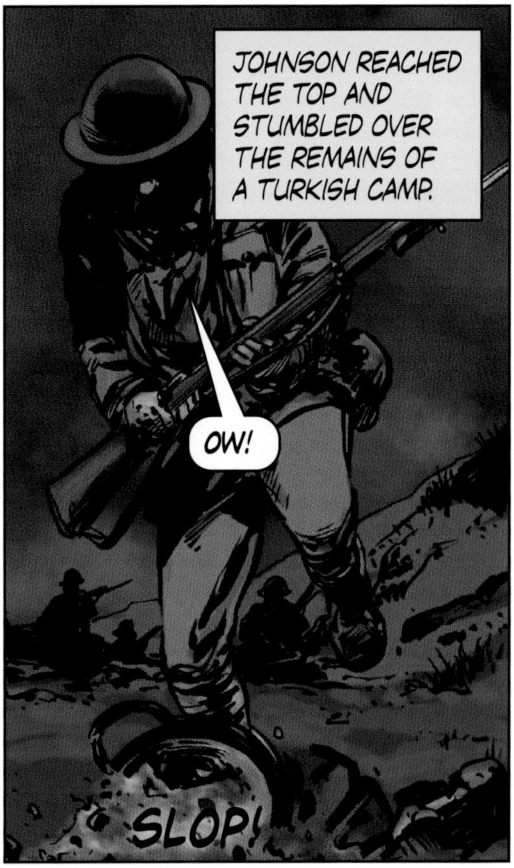
JOHNSON REACHED THE TOP AND STUMBLED OVER THE REMAINS OF A TURKISH CAMP.
OW!
SLOP!

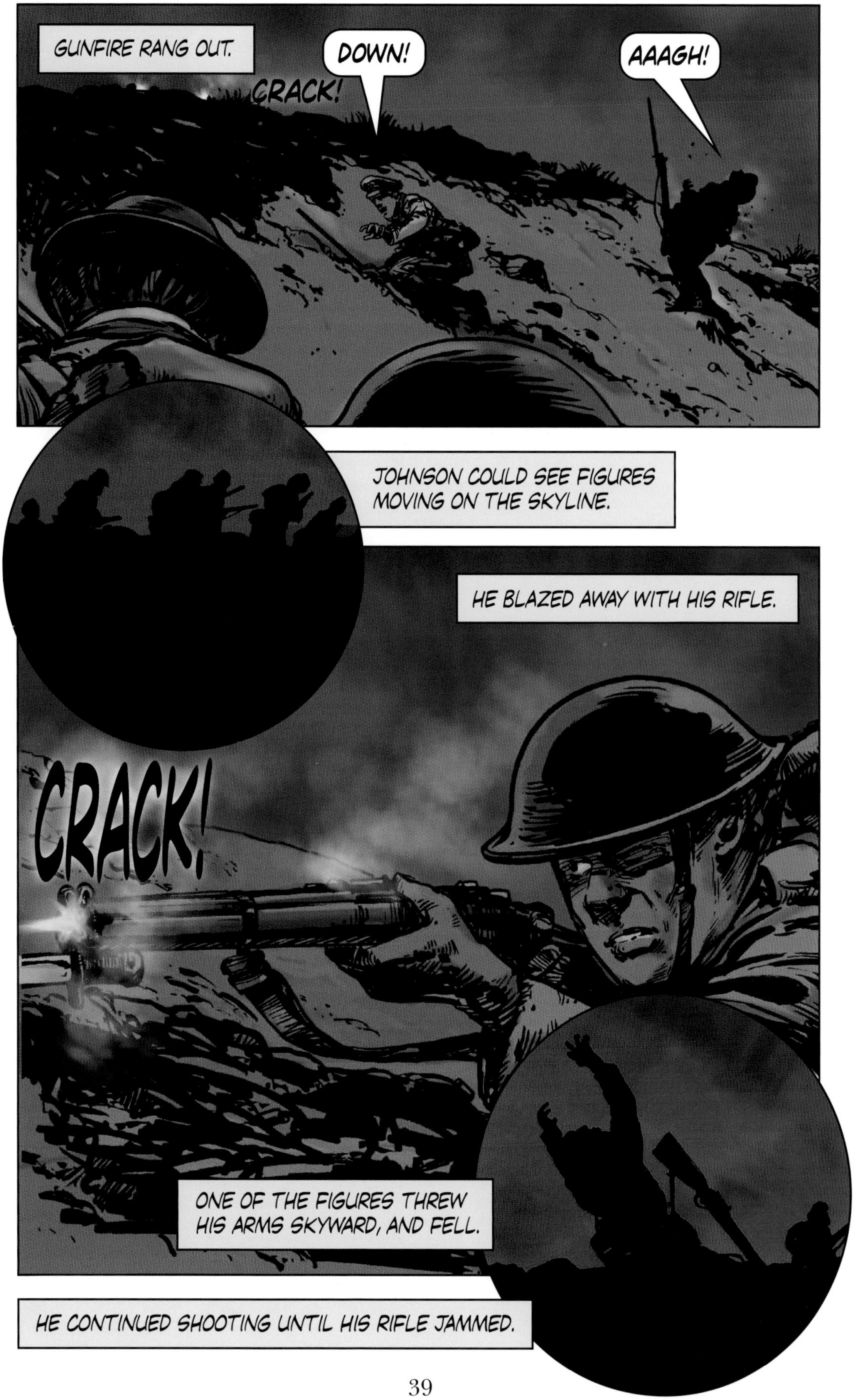
GUNFIRE RANG OUT.
CRACK!
DOWN!
AAAGH!
JOHNSON COULD SEE FIGURES MOVING ON THE SKYLINE.
HE BLAZED AWAY WITH HIS RIFLE.
CRACK!
ONE OF THE FIGURES THREW HIS ARMS SKYWARD, AND FELL.
HE CONTINUED SHOOTING UNTIL HIS RIFLE JAMMED.

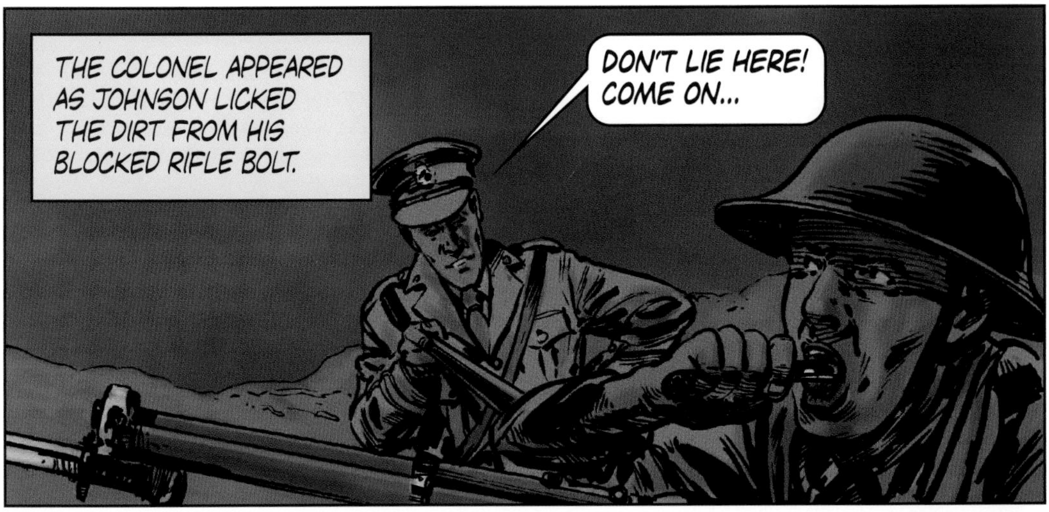
THE COLONEL APPEARED AS JOHNSON LICKED THE DIRT FROM HIS BLOCKED RIFLE BOLT.
DON'T LIE HERE! COME ON...

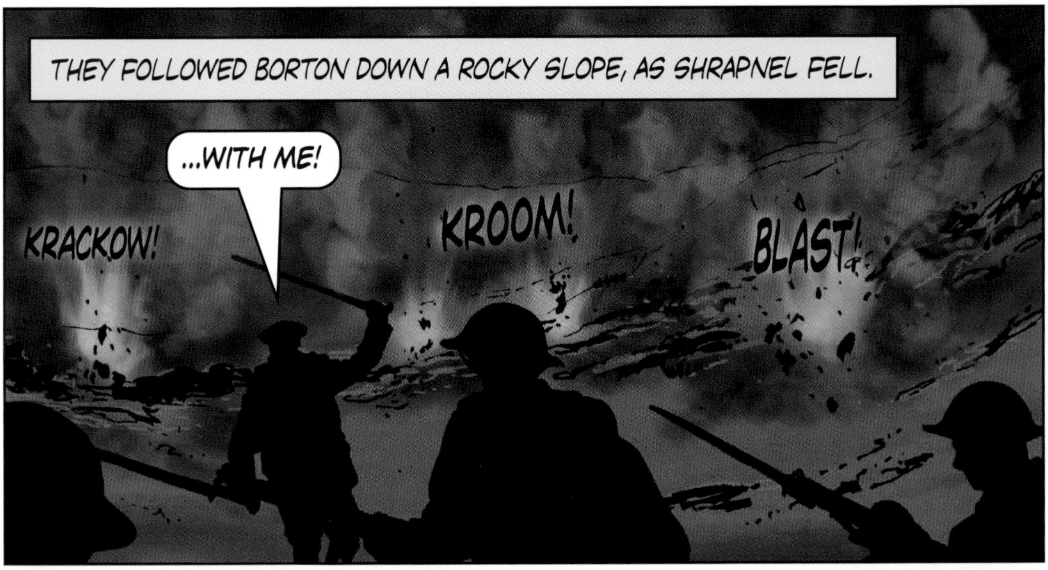
THEY FOLLOWED BORTON DOWN A ROCKY SLOPE, AS SHRAPNEL FELL.
...WITH ME!
KRACKOW!
KROOM!
BLAST!

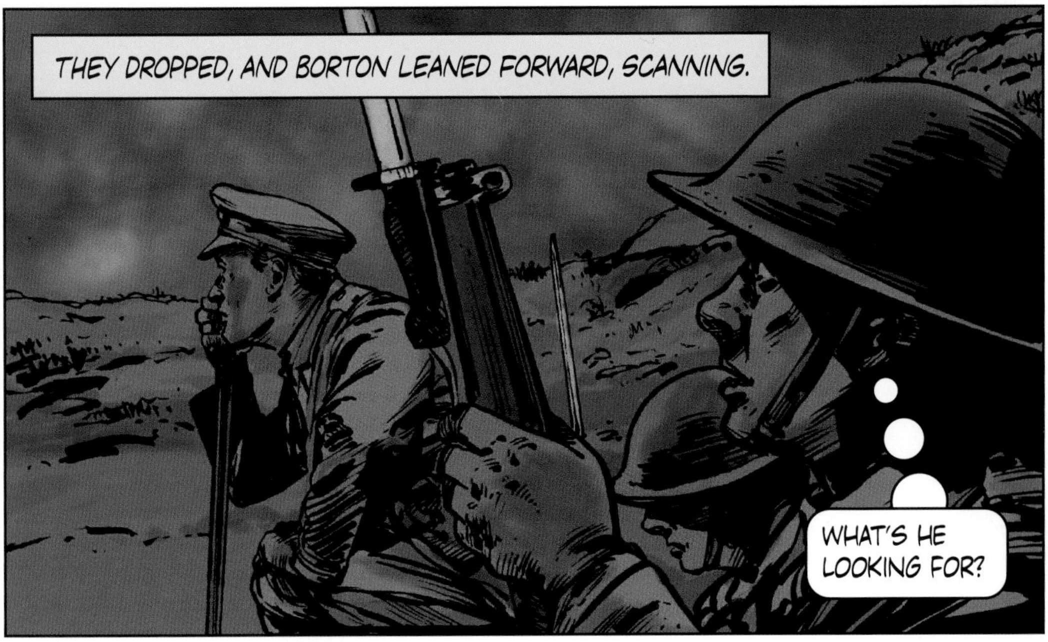
THEY DROPPED, AND BORTON LEANED FORWARD, SCANNING.
WHAT'S HE LOOKING FOR?

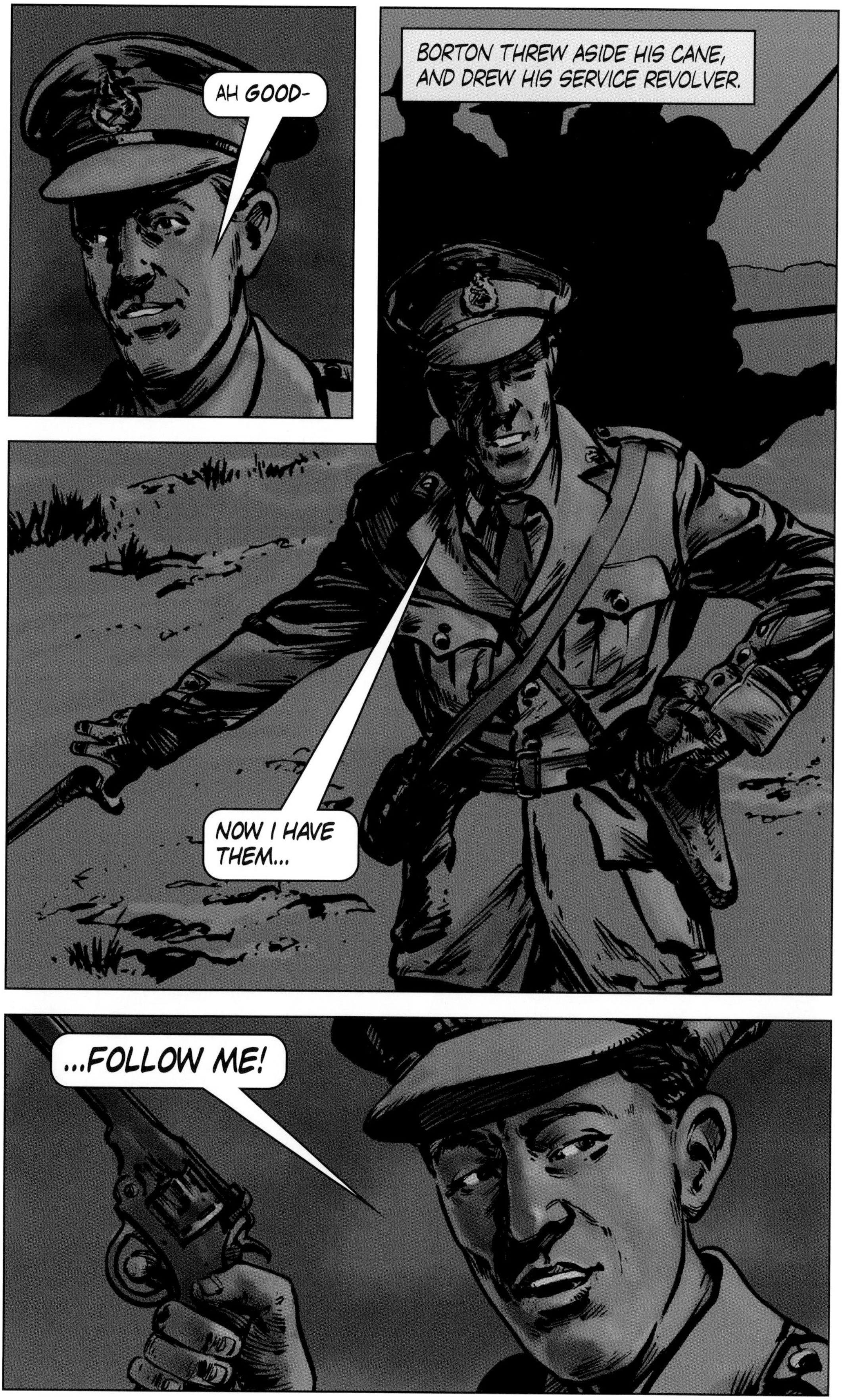
AH GOOD-
BORTON THREW ASIDE HIS CANE, AND DREW HIS SERVICE REVOLVER.
NOW I HAVE THEM...
...FOLLOW ME!

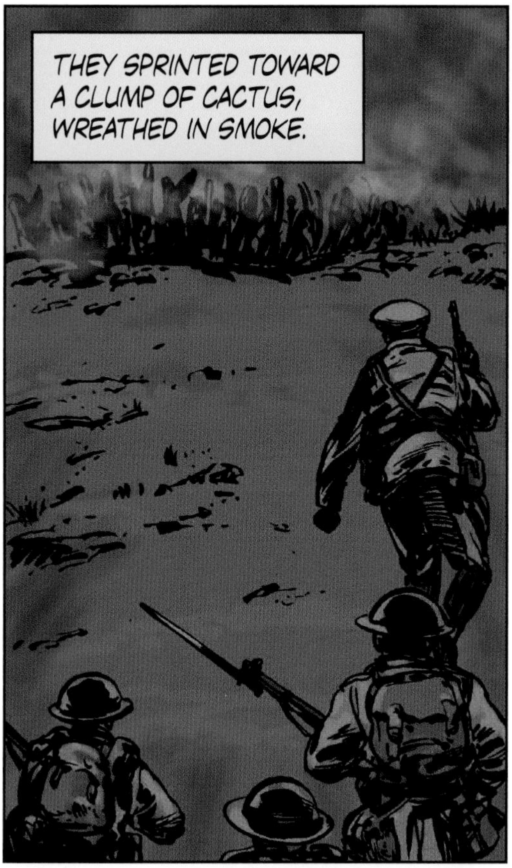
THEY SPRINTED TOWARD A CLUMP OF CACTUS, WREATHED IN SMOKE.

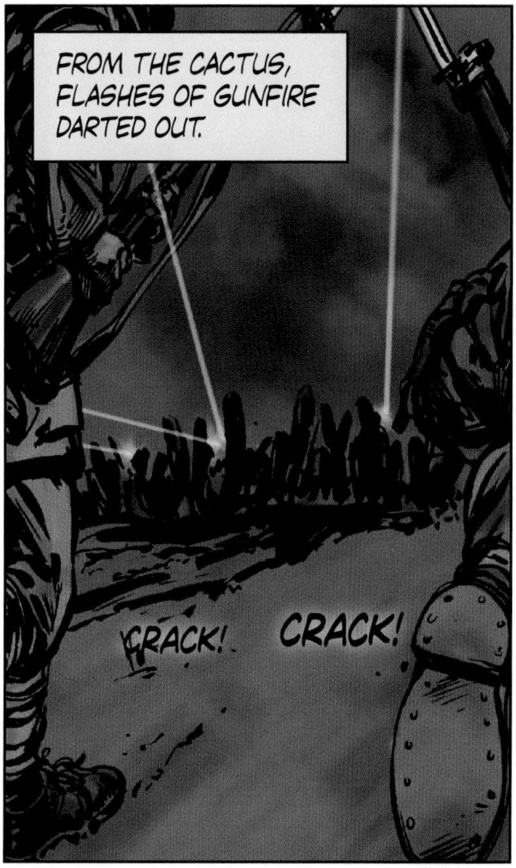
FROM THE CACTUS, FLASHES OF GUNFIRE DARTED OUT.
CRACK!
CRACK!

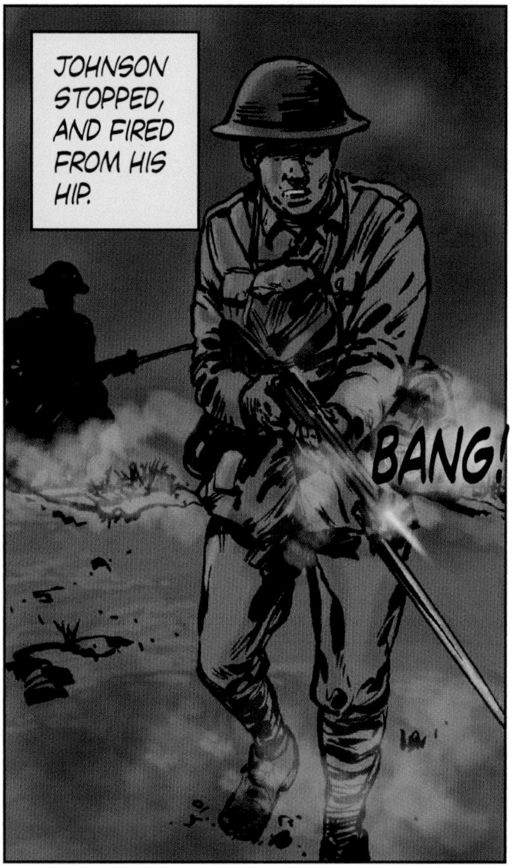
JOHNSON STOPPED, AND FIRED FROM HIS HIP.
BANG!

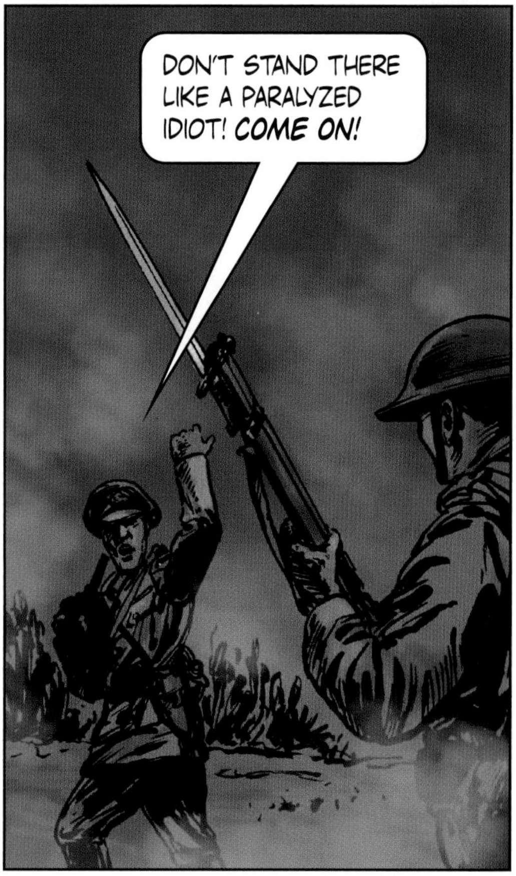
DON'T STAND THERE LIKE A PARALYZED IDIOT! COME ON!

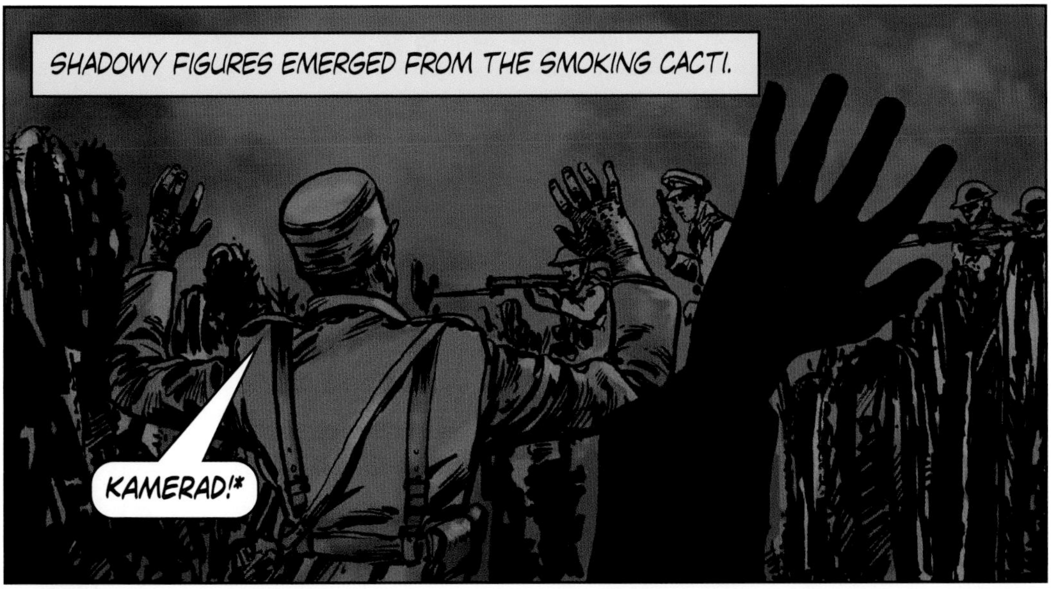
SHADOWY FIGURES EMERGED FROM THE SMOKING CACTI.
KAMERAD!*

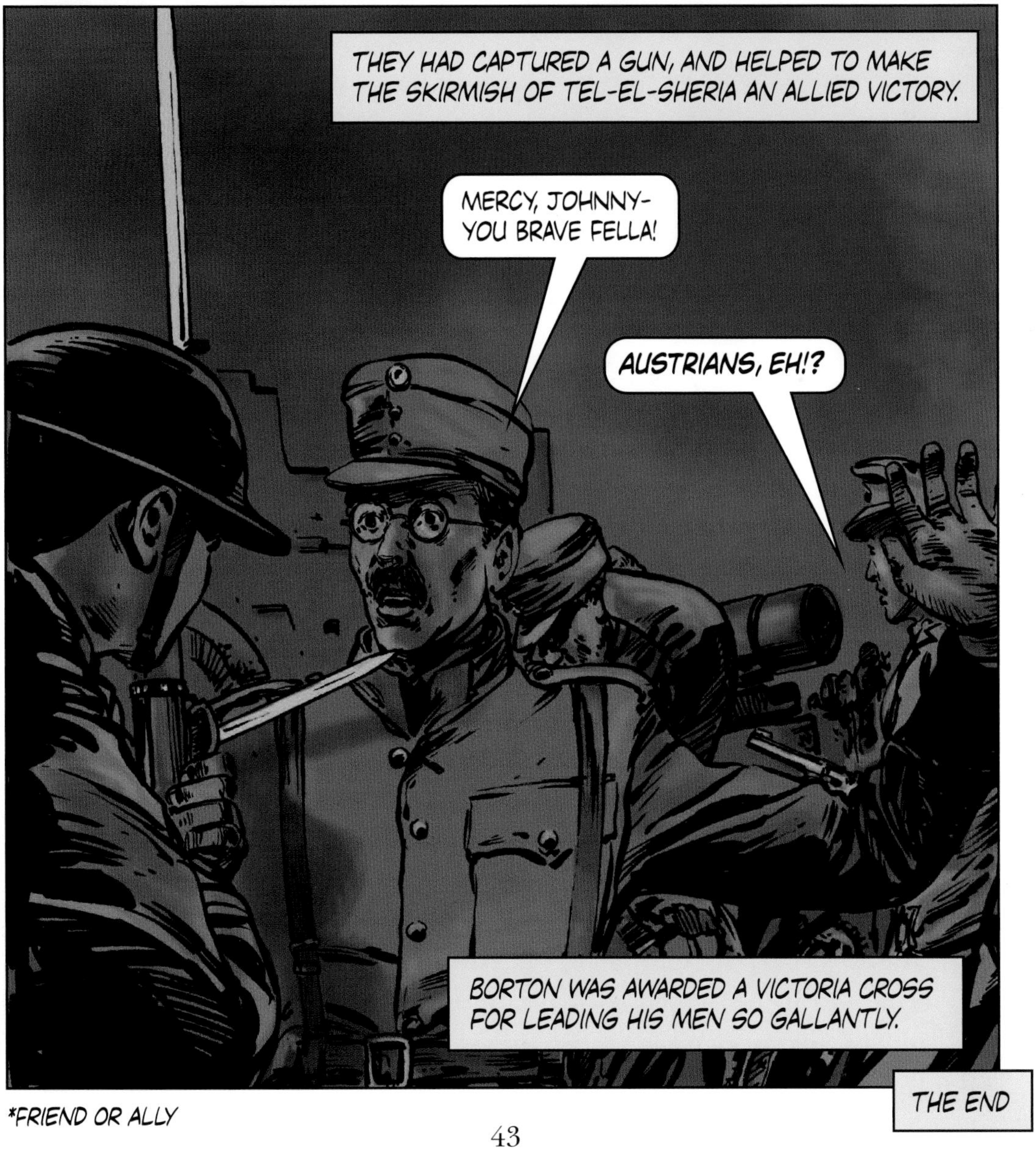
THEY HAD CAPTURED A GUN, AND HELPED TO MAKE THE SKIRMISH OF TEL-EL-SHERIA AN ALLIED VICTORY.
MERCY, JOHNNY- YOU BRAVE FELLA!
AUSTRIANS, EH!?
BORTON WAS AWARDED A VICTORIA CROSS FOR LEADING HIS MEN SO GALLANTLY.
THE END

*FRIEND OR ALLY

ALL WRAPPED UP

After Tel-El-Sheria the 20,000-strong Ottoman Army continued retreating northward across their whole line. Stiff fighting by rearguard units allowed them to fall back in good order.

Allenby entered Jerusalem on foot to show his respect for the Holy City.

A "Christmas Present"

Further cavalry charges were necessary, this time by British Yeoman regiments. Allenby kept the offensive moving, gaining 50 miles (80 kms) of territory in ten days. On December 9, Jerusalem fell. After the bloody stalemate of the Somme and other battles on the Western Front that year, the victory boosted British morale.

The Revolt Continues

Feisal's army had been resupplied by sea via Aqaba, from where they would aid the EEF's conquest of Northern Palestine. More tribes had joined the cause, which was bolstered by special forces, armored cars, and even mission air support

A British armored car in Palestine

from the Royal Flying Corps (RFC). Abdulla and his older brother, Ali, remained in Arabia to coordinate with the French army, attacking the railway, and besieging Medina. Feisal and Lawrence would cover Allenby's right flank, using their guerilla tactics.

THE UNDEFEATED

General Lettow-Vorbeck's surrender, pictured by an African artist

In East Africa Lettow-Vorbeck remained at large. The forces ranged against him were now colonial—his campaign could not affect the war's outcome. Three days after the armistice in Europe, on November 14, 1918, Lettow-Vorbeck received a telegram, ordering him to surrender at last.

A MASSACRE AT TAFAS

In mid-September 1918, Lawrence's force smashed the railway at Deraa, east of Nazareth. On September 27, a brigade of Turks, Germans, and Austrians, fleeing the EEF advance, attacked the village of Tafas, killing women and children. When the Arab army caught up with them, Lawrence ordered, "No prisoners!"—and none were taken.

The remains of Turkish wagons, bombed by the RFC at Meggido, 1918

MILITARY GENIUS AT MEGGIDO

The actions of Lawrence's force, although regrettable, aided Allenby's attempt to crush the Turks at nearby Meggido. Using an ancient Egyptian battle plan of 1480 B.C., Allenby had pushed his cavalry through a gap in the hills along the coast, and driven them inland to encircle the entire Turkish army, which fled, ending the war. For over two years Lawrence's Arab irregulars had tied up 30,000 enemy troops, greatly helping the victory.

Troopers of the Australian Light Horse entered Damascus on October 1, 1918. Thirty days later the armistice was signed.

45

GLOSSARY

affinity A liking or attraction to a person, thing, idea

aggressive Forceful, militant, menacing

ammunition The material fired from any weapon

armistice An agreement between opposing armies to stop fighting in order to discuss peace terms

besiege To crowd in upon; surround

cavalry A force of mounted soldiers who are trained to fight on horseback

daring Adventurous, brave, bold

detonate To explode something

dismount To alight from a horse

divert To turn aside from one path to follow a different course

epic Heroic and majestic; impressive and great

fierce Violent in force and intensity; wild or hostile

formidable Causing fear or apprehension

gallantry Great courage and bravery

gelignite An explosive material comprised of wood pulp, saltpetre and nitroglycerine or nitroglycol

guerilla Undercover, irregular forces, often attacking an enemy by surprise

infantry A unit of soldiers who fight on foot

Australian Light Horsemen being mobilized in 1914.

Lewis Gun An American-designed light machine gun used by the British in World War I

liaison The connection maintained by communications between units of armed forces, to ensure cooperation

massacre A general slaughter of persons

morale A person's emotional or mental condition with respect to confidence and cheerfulness during times of hardship

mosque A Muslim temple; a place of public worship

nomad A wanderer who has no permanent home

offensive A carefully planned military attack

pursue To follow closely in order to overtake

rebellion Defying or resisting an established authority

shrapnel Fragments from exploded ammunition

skirmish A fight between small bodies of troops

surrender To give up, abandon, yield

terrain A tract of land

trench A long, narrow hole dug in the ground to serve as a shelter from enemy fire or attack

triumph A significant success or achievement; victory

typhus An infectious disease characterized by exhaustion, headache, and red spots

wadi An Arabic word for valley or stream bed

wreathe To encircle, envelop or surround

Turkish machine gun corps on the Gaza line, near Beersheba, in 1917

47

INDEX